MAPPING YOUR FEARLESS FUTURE

a millennial's simple, easy guide to financial empowerment, confidence, and hope

PAYING OFF DEBT, STUDENT LOANS
MORTGAGES, BUDGETING
INSURANCE, RETIREMENT
AND MORE...

By Michael Kellermeyer, M.A.

Copyright © 2019 Michael Kellermeyer

Oldstyle Tales Media
Fort Wayne, Ind.

All rights reserved. No part of this publication may be reproduced, distributed, or transmitted in any form or by any means, including photocopying, recording, or other electronic or mechanical methods, without the prior written permission of the publisher, except in the case of brief quotations embodied in critical reviews and certain other noncommercial uses permitted by copyright law.

For permission requests, write to the publisher, addressed "Attention: Permissions Coordinator,"
at the address below.

Michael G. Kellermeyer
2424 N. Anthony Blvd.
Fort Wayne IN, 46805

— DEDICATED TO —

My wife, Kierstin, for believing in my potential, challenging me to be the best version of myself, and sharing my dreams, vision, and life…

— WITH THANKS TO —

My mom, for teaching me the importance of tithing,

my grandma, who listened to Larry Burkett and Dave Ramsey while I was growing up, and whose wedding present of books by these two men was the greatest blessing to our financial futures,

and to my cousin Brandon, whose dedication to self-improvement, reading, and understanding frequently came to mind as I wrote this…

— TABLE OF CONTENTS —

INTRODUCTION 7

PART ONE: YOUR FIRST STEPS TO FEARLESSNESS
   1. Making a Simple Budget 16
   2. Listing and Paying Off Debt 22
   3. Making Extra Money 25
   4. Keeping an Emergency Fund 28

PART TWO: TACKLING MAJOR DEBTS FEARLESSLY
   5. Credit Card Debt 34
   6. Vehicle Loans 40
   7. Student Loans 43
   8. Mortgages 48

PART THREE: PLANNING FOR A FEARLESS FUTURE
   9. Understanding and Getting a Nest Egg 52
   10. Understanding and Getting Insurance 70
   11. Understanding and Getting a Will 78

PART FOUR: WEATHERING THE FEARFUL STORMS
   12. Understanding and Avoiding Bankruptcy 84
   13. Understanding and Avoiding Foreclosure 88
   14. Understanding and Engaging Collectors 92

PART FIVE: HEALTHY HABITS FOR A FEARLESS FUTURE
   15. Having a Positive, Empowered Mindset 97
   16. Having an Encouraging, Edifying Community 104
   17. Having a Generous, Charitable Spirit 109

CONCLUSION 115
ONLINE RESOURCES 123
MUST-READ BOOKS 124

INTRODUCTION

"The oldest and strongest emotion of mankind is fear, and the oldest and strongest kind of fear is fear of the unknown."
— H. P. LOVECRAFT

"Who is going to harm you if you are eager to do [the right thing]? But even if you should suffer... 'Do not fear their threats; do not be frightened.'" – 1 PETER 3:13-14

☯

Fear can drive our choices. It can make us do desperate things. It can rob us of happiness and contentment, and urge us to compare our lives to others[1]. Fear is the greatest inhibitor of joy and the biggest bully of self-esteem. For almost ten years I worked as a college English professor, and my favorite part of that job was easing fear in my students because I knew what it felt like to be panicked and desperate. I loved calming them down when they were struggling to make a deadline and coaching them through the more confusing and frustrating portions of a challenging paper. It was viscerally relaxing to watch their faces unclench and their eyes light back up. They were afraid – of failing, of being lost, of being wrong – and I couldn't wait to replace that fear with hope.
  When you're a kid fear can be very abstract – monsters, sounds, nightmares – and when you're a teenager it can start to take the shape of identity issues – being uncool, being rejected, being unloved – but as we pass into young adulthood I've noticed so many of my friends find the ultimate boogeyman in their back-pockets: the gloomy

---

[1] "Are You Afraid to be Happy?" *Psychology Today* (July 2017)

labyrinth of finances[1]. It's not as scary when you're in college, even if you know that you'll be facing a lot of student loan debt: it's still the future-you's problem, and today you're able to eat cheap junk food and ask your parents for help and focus on passing biology quizzes that will have no bearing on your future. But when you get the first bill for a student loan or car loan or credit card payment, you suddenly feel that tightness in your throat and that dizziness in your head. It's not the future-you's problem, now – it's yours...

— MY OWN STORY OF FINANCIAL FEAR —

I went to college in 2006, just before the Great Recession, and chose a private school and a humanities degree, and by the time I graduated in 2010, I was staring down 35,000 in debt (and I was one of the lucky ones). I started grad school soon after, so I put off facing my debts for another three years, but in the fall of 2013, I made my first payment on nearly 40K in debt. It was $171, and the needle had hardly moved. In fact, with the interest I was racking up, I had probably taken a step backwards. But this was what you did, right? You paid the cost they asked for every month until it was all paid for. But how long would that be? Ten years? Twenty? Thirty? Still, it seemed unimportant that first year or two. I married my wife, Kierstin, two years later, and we bought our house one snowy March in 2015. We were homeowners, and since we lived in the Midwest in the low-cost-of-living city of Fort Wayne, in a cozy, blue-collar historic neighborhood, the mortgage was less than our rent at an apartment a quarter-mile away. It seemed perfect.

    Later that spring, the supposedly brand-new dryer gave out. This was pretty exasperating because the air conditioner didn't work either and the sellers had given us a choice: they could either pay to fix the air conditioner and take the new dryer and washer, or they could leave the appliances for us

---

[1] "5 Common Financial Fears and How to Overcome Them," *Bankrate*.com (October 31)

and skip over the A.C. We would rather have the laundry machines in a breezy Hoosier March, but now a steamy summer was coming and we were short a dryer only two months into our homeownership.

We went to Lowes and grabbed up a dryer on credit, assuming that that was that. Less than a month later the washer died on us (soon enough for us to buy a matching washing machine – not that it was of much comfort), and we had another appliance on credit. Then as June came, we realized we had no patio furniture to experience the beautiful summer nights with their fireflies and cicadas, so we ran out and snagged up a fire pit, backyard swing, and a bistro set.

At the time I was an adjunct professor, so I didn't get paid in the month of June or July, and even though I taught summer classes, the paycheck wouldn't show up until mid-August (and the next wouldn't show up until mid-September). And by July we realized that something was wrong. It was hard to keep up with our finances: simple purchases became stressful choices, trips to visit family turned into anxious fights about gas prices, and even though we would eat out six or seven times in the first two weeks of each month, we would suddenly be unable to afford a trip through the McDonald's drive-through by the third week.

It wasn't the first time we were afraid because of finances. I remember several very worrisome conversations (usually towards the end of a month) about our bank accounts, and I remember one or two tearful calls to my parents, asking for prayer and the loan of some money for rent. But I'd thought we were beyond that now – we were married and homeowners! Why didn't this feel right yet?

— FINDING FINANCIAL FEARLESSNESS —

For their wedding present to us, my mom's parents gifted us two books by financial gurus: one by Larry Burkett, and one by Dave Ramsey. Both had never been opened, but one sweltering, July night – with both of us frightened and desperate – I suggested seeing what their advice was. I read the Burkett book and Kierstin read the Dave Ramsey book, and by the first of August we had plotted out our first budget. We had just wanted to be able to have less stress, but what we read changed everything: not only did we have a defense against worry, we had an offense against mediocrity. With a $50,000 combined income, almost $70,000 in debt, and a mortgage to pay, we began a journey that would lead to our becoming debt-free in less than two years. Today we have an emergency fund to stave off any conceivable surprise costs, we don't buy anything we can't cash flow, and we feel ultra-comfortable telling people "no" when we can't afford to eat out with them or visit them across state (not because we were strapped for cash, but because we would be if we didn't learn to say "no" when we didn't have the money at hand).

     As a result, we felt fear melt away and fearlessness take its place – not arrogance or over-confidence or cocksure swagger. No, this was a cool, calm, collected sigh of relief and hope. Do this with me right now: let the air slowly out of your lungs in a low, steady gush, pause for two beats, and – now – fill your lungs full of cool, clean air. Feel it expanding your chest with life and security, rising through your nose, lightening your head and calming your heartbeat. Your eyes feel lighter and your blood thinner. Now exhale again – *gussshhhh…* – pause two beats – and inhale – and exhale… The coolness of life and hope expands through you… This is the physical feeling of fearlessness. It isn't tight or tense or worrisome. It isn't bent or curled, not clenched or pulsing. It's open and expansive…

— FEARING THE UNKNOWN —

Five years ago I started a side business publishing annotated and illustrated editions of classic horror fiction: Dracula, Frankenstein, Dr. Jekyll and Mr. Hyde; ghost stories, murder mysteries, weird tales. Looking back on it, I think I've realized that fear has always been something that resonated with me. Stories about ghosts and goblins take the abstract, frightful parts of life and craft them into physical apparitions – things you can see and try to understand. Even though it might sound crazy, I think that financial troubles are far more terrifying than a vampire or werewolf: vampires have hearts that you can drive stakes into and werewolves have shaggy hides that can be pierced with silver bullets, but what can kill $125,000 in student loan debt when you're working as a barista and you just had your car repoed? You can exorcise a demon and arrest a murderer, but what can you do when your child has medical bills, your house is being foreclosed on, and your husband walks out on you?

The 20th century master of weird fiction, H. P. Lovecraft, once said that the "oldest and strongest emotion of mankind is fear, and the oldest and strongest kind of fear is fear of the unknown[1]." The creator of the extraterrestrial sea-demon Cthulhu knew what he was saying when he recognized the existential power of fear and its primary source: a lack of knowledge. Things are immediately less frightening when we understand their dimensions – their limitations and weaknesses – and financial debt is no different than a werewolf in this capacity: learn its vulnerabilities, and it will stop having power over your choices. You'll sleep better, get up easier, laugh more, and smile oftener. Instead of being thrown into a panic when a tire goes out, you'll be temporarily miffed: "it turns a crisis into an inconvenience[2]" when you have no debt, an emergency fund over $10,000, growing investments in well-researched IRA's, and a flexible-but-intentional plan for the future.

Banish fear from your home. Welcome confidence and empowerment inside and watch rampant hope bloom in your heart like a cherry blossom opening up to the April sun. Replace the tension of worry with the comfort of peace.

---

[1] "Supernatural Horror in Literature," H. P. Lovecraft (1927)
[2] "What if Your Emergency Fund Can't Cover Your Emergency?" *Dave Ramsey Blog*

Experience the release of anxiety as awareness warms up your spirit's frosty chambers. Fearlessness doesn't mean naïveté or arrogance or nonchalance: it means having a plan and knowing what you will do when troubles come. And they will: this month my wife and I had to pay over $800 in taxes, had a $1,500 unexpected purchase, had a $200 furnace-repair bill, over $200 in unplanned deductibles, and this was all after we made a $400 purchase that we thought would be our only unusual cost that month. It was annoying. It meant cancelling a bed-and-breakfast stay we'd planned on taking next month, and changing plans to visit my parents this week, but that was it. We didn't even need to pull anything out of our emergency fund and – I'll be happy to be transparent – we are solidly middle-middle-class, making five figures, and although we can envision making six as time goes on, for now five figures is more than enough. It's enough because we know what our goals are, we know what they'll cost, and we know what we need to make to pay for them upfront. Our family doesn't spend more than we make, we don't take out debt, and we don't let fear be our houseguest. Fear has no place in a house ruled by hope.

— SWITCHING CLASSROOMS —

After becoming debt free, we had a wild year of change: my wife started working at our very lofty, high-churchy Lutheran church that January, but by July she left her job, and we left our largely upper-class, white-collar, Left-leaning congregation and began attending a multi-generational, multi-cultural, politically-mixed, nondenominational church with a wide range of socio-economic representation. The culture shock of spending time with such a diverse mix of people was fascinating: in our previous, upper-class congregation, we had been decidedly young and decidedly poor, but here, surrounded by people from the whole spectrum of age, race, wealth, and culture, I realized just how diverse peoples' financial experiences could be. Here, instead of being surrounded by greying white people with six figure incomes and new cars, I was exposed to a wide range of needs, hopes, dreams, and goals. It inspired me to come alongside them and help them achieve those dreams.

The previous year I had been promoted to a full-time lecturer at my college, and was inducted into the shadowy background of higher education – it was a shocking and disappointing experience. I knew that colleges naturally survived by accepting student tuition, but I wasn't aware of just how irresponsible, dehumanizing, and callous it truly was. Colleges like this predatorily lure students – often from lower class urban or rural communities – into paying tens of thousands of dollars for impractical degrees, and while they genuinely hope that they will graduate, many of these students were never college material to begin with. Before their four years were up, 31% of them would drop out[1], often with an average of $37,000 in debt[2]. It – along with the increasingly manic culture of American universities[3], replete with trigger warnings, finger-snapping, safe spaces, and identity politics – convince me to change professions by the end of the spring   semester that May.

I was concerned about this transition, but resolved that it had to happen. Before long, however, my two experiences at church and work blended together: instead of helping Big Higher-Ed prey on young people with flimsy promises and irresponsible lending, I decided to help people who had been beaten down by financial fear. People like my wife and I, the people at our church, and the students in my old classrooms; people bent by the weight of student loans, car payments, consumer debt, foreclosures, repossessions, and bankruptcies. So I left my job teaching hungover college athletes and started teaching these groups of people – frightened, desperate, and holding onto hope – instead.

Pulling together the lessons from my grandparents' books, hundreds of hours' worth of listening to financial coaching sessions, and my completion of Financial Coach Master

---

[1] "College Completion Rates are Still Disappointing," *Forbes* (Dec 2017)
[2] "Student Loan Debt Statistics in 2018," *Forbes* (June 2018)
[3] *The Coddling of the American Mind*, Greg Lukianoff and Jonathan Haidt (2018)

Training, I've designed this book to make the more intense elements of personal finance simple and digestible. What I've come to know – and what I want you to learn – is that there are six things you must do to be financially confident:

1. **Pay off and avoid debt at all costs**
2. **Regularly operate a specific monthly budget**
3. **Maintain a robust emergency fund for unexpected costs**
4. **Invest wisely in select IRA's with a guiding, proven investor**
5. **Have the appropriate instruments of insurance in place**
6. **Cultivate a spirit of gratitude, generosity, and humility**

Throughout this book I'll breakdown all six steps: we'll talk about how to start a budget, make a plan for paying off debt, and how to become debt-free; we'll discuss the critical importance of establishing a rainy day fund, getting the right (not the wrong) kind of insurance, and putting a will in place for your loved ones; we'll discuss investing – who to trust with your investments and what to expect, and we'll talk about the positive attitude that 97% of American millionaires (1/3 of whom make less than six figures annually) cultivate in their own lives[1]: an attitude of optimism, self-control, gratitude, and outrageous charity.

    This book is intended to be a silver bullet for your financial fears: it's small, simple, and short, but it packs a wallop. If you're going through lots of financial chaos right now, I'd recommend seeing a financial coach to help you wade through the mess, but for the time being, this can act as a compass in the swamp, pointing you towards good choices, wise planning, and a fearless future.

Michael Kellermeyer
Fort Wayne, March 2019

---

[1] *Everyday Millionaires*, Chris Hogan (2019)

PART ONE
— Your First Steps to Fearlessness —

Simple budgeting, Listing and paying off debt,
and earning extra money.

CHAPTER 1.
— Making a Simple Budget —

"Adults devise a plan and follow it; children do what feels good." – DAVE RAMSEY

"The plans of the diligent lead to profit, as surely as haste leads to poverty." – PROVERBS 21:5

Lindsey was a carefree 23 year-old fresh out of college with $48,000 in debt and an entry-level teaching job making $29,000. She was kind, spontaneous, impulsive, and fun to be around, and even though she didn't worry very often, after she got a loan for a $18,000 car, she started to realize that something had to change, and it was the worst thing she could imagine: she had to get a plan for her money. Lindsey wasn't big on planning – it was part of her identity to be untethered to the future, but that was what motivated her to find help: she realized that the choices she was making in the present would determine what she could and could not afford to do in the future. She needed to get a budget in place if she was going to pay off debt, start investing, and build wealth. Wealth wasn't money – wealth was freedom to choose what kind of life she wanted to have...

&

Budgeting is the most powerful element to healthy finances, and while it may seem complicated at first, it's also one of the easiest skills to master once you've gotten started. Almost everyone I know or have heard of who's gotten out of debt has cited budgeting – along with purpose and sticking to a plan – as one of the top three reasons for success. So why is budgeting so important? The short answer is, when you don't have control of your outgoing income, you can't expect it to work the way you hope: "hoping" something will happen isn't a wise way to plan your future.

— BEGINNING YOUR BUDGETING HABIT —

What budgeting amounts to is gathering up all of your expected monthly income, and then making a list of every expense you plan on having that month. Begin with the essentials: food, rent/mortgage payments, utilities, transportation, clothing, and household staples. Now keep in mind – to begin with – "food" means different things depending on where your finances are (ditto with "clothing," "housing," "utilities," etc.): if you're in a lot of debt, "food" might mean macaroni and hotdogs and fried potatoes for a while, but as your finances improve, you can spend more (or if you're willing to tighten the budget on less important items, you can spread that money over to food in order to buy better quality produce.

Once these essential items have been decided (e.g., $600 for food, $1,000 for utilities, $580 for rent, and $200 for clothing out of a $6,000/month income), it's time to break the leftovers into what we will loosely call Lifestyle, Savings, Giving, and Debt. If you're in debt right now, I'd urge you to spend most of that on paying your debts down – instead of paying minimums for fifteen years, be aggressive and watch that debt get vaporized in two[1]! This is critical, as we'll talk about later, if you want to avoid accruing a ton of interest, and want to free up your disposable income for Savings and Lifestyle and Giving. So let's talk about that six-grand income example: we've put aside $2,000 for basic needs, which leaves four; do you really need to spend most of that on

---

[1] "The Debt Snowball Method is the Most Effective Way to Pay Off Debt," *CNBC Money* (March 2018)

eating out, travel, movies, subscriptions, clothes, and iPhones when you're barely making it month to month? No chance. You might decide that half of that can go to debt – or even more! If you're nervous about that, start smaller, but try increasing your payments every month: see how much you can pay! When my wife and I were getting out of debt, it was an exciting experience every time we cranked up the number of dollars flowing out because it felt like increasing the weights in a workout or the miles on a run (we do neither of those things, but I'm guessing here): we could feel the debt shrinking and were willing to pay a lot to dump it even earlier than expected.

— PLANNING GIVING AND SPENDING —

The next thing to decide is how much you're going to give: even if you're in debt you should exercise generosity, because that's the difference between turning into a miser once you're debt-free and being charitable and financially healthy. In our house we do this by tithing to our church, giving to charities, and – most importantly – helping folks out when we hear about a need in our community. Some people will disagree with this, but I would recommend making Giving a part of your monthly budget every month, although I don't recommend going over ten percent while you're still in debt (but afterwards, if you can afford to give it, then feel free to be generous!). If you personally don't think you can afford to give at this point, don't feel pressured, but use that as a motivation to get out of debt: generous people are happier people, and if you can't afford to be generous, it's difficult to be happy.

The last section to focus on is Lifestyle: I don't recommend that you do any Savings of any kind while you're getting out of debt. If you power through your debts in a year or two, you'll be free to save and invest afterward, but doing it now will only delay your freedom[1]. So on to Lifestyle: this is the stuff that we cut back as much as possible while we're in debt, and the stuff that we look forward to restoring once we're free. Categories here would be things like pet grooming, movies, travel, extra

---

[1] "How to Get Out of Debt with the Debt Snowball Plan," *Dave Ramsey Blog*

clothing, subscriptions, new technology, new furniture, and really, new *anything*. At this point, we have room for some of those things some of the time, but really try to cut back until you're finally out of financial bondage.

— ACTUALLY DOING IT —

So what does this look like practically? For one thing, I know some people like to write this out by hand, and that's great, but my wife and I recommend that everyone try out www.everydollar.com, first: it's a free budgeting website where you fill these categories out and then subtract the money anytime you buy something or pay a bill or loan. So you just got groceries? Open the app up or login online and subtract the $584 you spent. By the way, you have leftover money there, and if you still have it by the end of the month, you can either put that toward debt or add that to another category, or just let next month's food budget be $616. You just bought new socks? When you get back to the car, before you pull out of the parking lot even, subtract the $5.67 from Clothing. You just gave $120 to your church for tithe? Remove that from your Giving fund before you head home. It sounds tedious, but make sure you keep up with it, and you'll suddenly realize that you have way more money than you realized. What's really eating up your income? Probably eating out, entertainment, and impulse shopping. These things are totally fine when you're out of debt, but if you aren't, you're probably suffering because you aren't telling your impulses "no."

    So now I'd like to show you a before-and-after example budget, just to give you an idea of what yours might look like, but keep in mind, everyone has different needs and hobbies and expenses, so yours will have some extra categories and probably won't include all of the ones in this model:

IN-DEBT BUDGET…	DEBT-FREE BUDGET!
Food – 600	Food – 600
Utilities – 1000	Utilities – 1000
Rent – 580	Rent – 580
Clothing – 200	Clothing – 200
Debt – 3000	Savings – 900
Giving – 200	Giving – 600
Entertainment – 20	Entertainment – 60
Pets – 50	Pets – 70
Health/Wellness – 100	Health/Wellness – 150
Haircuts – 100	Haircuts – 150
Travel / Gas – 50	Travel / Gas – 300
Misc. – 100	Gifts – 70
	Eating Out – 120
	Shopping – 500
	Garden – 80
	DIY – 80
	Furniture – 200
	Misc. – 120

You might wonder what you should do if you have a sudden expense or if something changes. That's easy: you just agree to adjust what's left in the budget and move it around to accommodate the change. Now remember, this doesn't mean you get to take out a new debt or spend money you don't have, and this is why – as we'll see – it's always important to have around $2,000 in an "getting-out-of-debt" emergency fund (something you never, ever, ever spend except in emergencies, and something you focus all of your attention on building back up any time you need to use it)[1]. If there's $60 left in haircuts and you need money for a broken toaster, you can decide: do we replace the toaster with haircut money and just leave it a little rustic-looking for a month, or is there another area we can take the money from, OR, can we wait a month to get a new toaster.

---

[1] "Why an Emergency Savings Fund is so Important," www.advantageccs.org

Having a budget and sticking to it is the number one key to getting out of debt and having a fearless future. If you have a partner, you need to start every month with a brand new budget. A lot of the items will just roll over, but you still need to take the time to consider them: in May you might need an extra $30 in gas money to visit the family for Mother's Day; in July you might foresee the need to replace your car's A.C. fluid and need a little extra in maintenance; in December you already know that you're going to need an extra $400 for Christmas presents... You get the picture. Every first of the month (or the last day or day before last, if you want to get an early start) you should plan your finances, adjust the budget, and spit-shake on it: no unplanned purchases unless you agree to take that money from another area (and then agree that that money is now "spent").

When you have a budget, your money obeys your wishes, not the other way around. So, so, so many times I can remember it being midway through the month and my wife and I growing pale and sweaty realizing that we are going to have to cancel a get together across state with friends, or ask my parents to lend us gas money to make it home for Easter, or – and this happened – realize that one of us is not going to get a birthday gift that year (it was me, but I deserved it because it was my impulse purchase earlier that month that robbed us of that choice). And that's what this all boils down to: choice. Budgets give you freedom because they offer you choices, and if you follow a budget, you can "choose" to have the money for a gift that month, or gas money for visiting friends, or a little extra to go out to dinner with your in-laws[1]. But when you rob Peter to pay Paul, you'll find that more often than not, you've limited your choices and you have to say "no" to something that you might have been able to say "yes" to if you'd had a plan going into the month. Budgets seem restricting, but they're really about freedom – freedom to choose to say no to somethings now, so that you can say yes to something more important to you later on.

---

[1] "Budgeting Isn't a Bad Word," www.rachelcruze.com

CHAPTER 2.
— Listing and Paying Off Debt —

"We live in a debt-ridden society that is now virtually dependent on a constant expansion of debt to keep the economy going… it is easy to rationalize not paying a debt, especially when one's financial situation seems to be out of control." – LARRY BURKETT

"Free yourself [from debt] like a gazelle from the hand of the hunter, like a bird from the snare of the fowler." – PROV. 6:5

After Lindsey made her first budget, she realized that it wasn't enough to take control of the present – she had to fix mistakes from the past if she was going to have any margin. Making minimum payments on 48K would take years and years to complete. Even though she didn't like restricting her life to a plan, she realized that nonchalance with debt in the present would lead to a future of limitations. She made a list of her debts – three student loans of 4K, 19K, and 25K – and her car loan of $18,000. The car had been hers for a year, and was now worth $16,000, but she made the decision to sell it and buy a ten year old car from a retiree for three grand. Within two months she had paid off the smallest student loan and the balance of her car loan…

෴

This chapter is very simple to write because the *solution* to paying off debts is simple: focus on paying it off by chucking as much money as you can at it, pay them off in order of size, and don't sweat the interest rate. Lots of people will consider this completely counterintuitive, but if your plan is to get out of debt as soon as possible, interest rates won't matter[1]. See, you should worry about interest rates if you're planning on being in debt for five, seven, ten years or more, allowing that interest to build and build[2]. But if you focus on paying the debt off, most people can do this in less than five years. Let's say you make $60,000 and have $40,000 in debt; if you live on $40,000 and spend the left-overs on the debt, you're done in two years. If you make the same but have $140,000 in debt, then it's obviously time to get some odd jobs, to sell stuff, and to donate a lot of blood, but even then, let's say that cranks your income to $75,000 and you live on only $25,000: you're done in less than three years. Is it fun? Do you have an envious Instagram feed? No, but who cares what other folks think of your personal choices? Be you and be debt-free. How about if you're making $25,000 but have a $15,000 car and $20,000 in student loans? Sell that car and get a used one for about four grand from Craigslist, or use mass transit if you live in a city. Now that debt is down to $21,000, but you can't be expected to have lots of wiggle room with your income, so start tutoring, delivering pizzas, working at Target, or cutting lawns on the side and I'll bet you can scrape together $1,000 a month, bringing that income up to $32,000. Pour all of that – and a little extra – into the debt, and it's out of town in less than two years.

    So if you go hard and fast with debt, the interest rate isn't going to add that much to your debt, but discouragement sure will: if you have four loans that are $500, $5,000, $15,000, and $50,000 in number and you try to take out the biggest one first, it's obvious that it will be a few years before you can claim a victory, and that can be very depressing and defeating, so instead of plugging away, you give up[3]. See, paying off debts is about small, incremental

---

[1] "The 'Snowball Approach' to Debt," Northwestern University – Kellogg (2012)
[2] "The Snowball Method is the Most Effective Way to Pay Off Debt," *CNBC Money*, (March 2018)
[3] "The 'Snowball Approach' to Debt," Northwestern University – Kellogg (2012)

victories that encourage you and prove that you're capable of finding confidence and fearlessness. While you might accrue some debt from high interest rates, you'll make that up by getting excited when you pay off the $500 loan in one month (yay!), the $5,000 one in ten weeks (yay!!), the $15,000 one in six months (YAY!!!), and wallop that $50,000 monster in two and a half years (HUZZAH!!!). This kind of intentional intensity is way more effective because it's about the psychology, not the math: emotion motivates people to act when logic gives them room to wait, change their mind, give up, and be a slave to fear[1].

— SO, HOW DO YOU PAY OFF DEBT? —

1. List every debt you have, ranking from the smallest, most kickable one, all the way up to your monster

2. Pour as much cash as you can spare on the smallest one and celebrate as you watch it melt away like a snowball in July

3. Move up the ladder and follow the pattern

4. Don't sweat the interest rates unless you plan to get tired and give up because you're watching months and years go by without any victories scored

---

[1] "The Psychological Trick that Will Help You Pay Off Debt Fast," Psychology Today (September 2015)

CHAPTER 3.
— Making Extra Money —

"My grandmother used to say "there's a great place for you to go when you're broke – to work!'" – DAVE RAMSEY

"The soul of the sluggard craves and gets nothing, while the soul of the diligent is richly supplied." – PROVERBS 13:4

Lindsey now had a total of $44,000 in debt, a $29,000 income, and a dream to be in control of her life. She learned that there are basically two elements that control how fast you get out of debt: how much you can make, and how much you spend – the income and the outgo. As an elementary school teacher she had a lot on her plate, but she was excited to watch the debt disappear so that she could start planning for a future of travel and adventure. She decided to start giving swimming lessons over the summer and took on two part time jobs: one at Starbucks and one at Barnes and Noble. That summer she was able to rake together $15,000 dollars between the three gigs, and when school started up in August, she began babysitting for couples from her church and raking leaves for her elderly neighbors in October. She was shocked – and delighted – when she found herself debt free by the following Fourth of July – instead of fifteen years of minimal payments, she had completed the daunting chore in a breakneck fifteen months…

☙

A lot of people feel helpless when they get into debt because they view their income as fixed: if you make $32,000 but have $60,000 in student debt and are only making minimal payments, it's true that that could take a decade to pay off. But you aren't helpless: when you need money and you live in country with a free market, you can always go outside and trade your labor for capital.

Some of the best ways to make extra dough are the simplest: babysitting, raking leaves, mowing lawns, shoveling snow, picking up groceries, cooking meals for the homebound, housesitting or pet-sitting, cleaning gutters, fixing a broken shelf, planting flowers, making cookies, dog-walking, etc. None of those require a college degree or a criminal background check or a job interview: just spread the word on social media or ask friends if they or their friends could use help with any of these tasks. Usually people will part with twenty-to-fifty bucks for one of these chores[1]. Do one a day and that's $100 if you give yourself a weekend, do this for four weeks and one or two weekends thrown in, and that's $500. Do this for a year and your income went from $32,000 to $38,000. Pick up one part time job in addition to this – say, doing some light work at Lowes, Target, a garden center, a bakery, a coffeehouse, a tutoring center, a library, a bookstore, a restaurant, or subbing for a school – and you're likely to make at least $800 - $1,000 a month. On the conservative side, that brings your income up to around $50,000, then, and your $60,000 loan is paid off in three years if you live on $30,000 – easily two years if you're aggressive!

Now, I admit, I'm a creative type, and I'm introverted, and I'm a little too proud for my own good, so some of these jobs might sound anxiety-producing to people like me. Fair enough. But creative types have the most marvelous invention of the modern age at their disposal: the internet[2]! Sell your crafts, jewelry, clothes, or artwork on Etsy and you can still probably scrape together that $100 a week – more if you invest time and effort into it – and you can give music or art lessons as a side gig, tutor at a school or college, or find work at one of the more introvert friendly jobs like a bookstore, coffeehouse, or museum.

---

[1] "25 Creative Ways to Make $100 Every Day," *Gathering Dreams* (March 2019); "13 Ways to Make $17 or More Babysitting," *Frugal for Less*
[2] "30 Online Side Jobs that can Make You $500 this Week," www.ratracerebellion.com (May 2017)

You can also start a website and try to attract advertisers (hard work), or use it to sell your products to a wider audience of individual consumers (easier work). What do you love? What do you know a lot about? Do you speak another language or know how to play an instrument or have a knack for math, history, or science? You're a commodity, then! Capitalize on your skills and abilities, and watch as people trade you dollars for your insight and intellect. Start a Facebook page or an Instagram account and see for yourself!

LIST OF SIDE HUSTLES YOU CAN CONSIDER:
- Tutoring in a subject you know well
- Giving lessons in music, art, dance, or sports
- Walking dogs / checking on cats / housesitting
- Babysitting for a couple with a weekly date night
- Raking leaves / shoveling snow / cutting grass
- Helping with gardening or landscaping
- Cleaning gutters / doing odd job repairs
- Selling clothes / books / jewelry on eBay
- Starting a craftsy Etsy store
- Selling art online or at local markets
- Selling fresh veggies / flowers / jarred food / soap / handmade items at a farmer's market
- Checking on, or spending time with the elderly
- Giving workshops in a skill you're great at
- Having or hosting a neighborhood garage sale
- Making and selling woodworking projects
- Making and selling homemade beauty products
- Starting a home décor / home organizing / or life coaching service
- Getting a part time job at a local business
- Getting licensed as a notary or tax preparer
- Take a class to become certified in a marketable skill without spending thousands for a degree
- Give baking / cooking lessons
- Deliver pizzas / take-out
- Open your house as an Airbnb
- Donate blood

CHAPTER 4.
— Keeping an Emergency Fund —

"Annual income £20, annual expenditure £19.06 result happiness. Annual income £20, annual expenditure £20.06 result misery." – CHARLES DICKENS

"The wise store up choice food and oil, but fools gulp theirs down." – PROVERBS 21:20

Liam and Kaitlyn had been married for two months when their air conditioning went out in July... in New Mexico. The repair cost $1,200, and their bank account had $300 in it – a comparatively rich amount for a couple who routinely found themselves with 50 or 60 bucks left in their checking. They didn't have a savings account, so they happily paid for the repair with a credit card. Then Liam's $8,000 truck went off the road in a sandstorm and was totaled. Instead of buying a comparable truck with the insurance check, they got one three times as expensive on credit, and put the $300 in towing and wrecking costs on their card. That August they felt like they were getting their bearings again when Kaitlyn broke a tooth riding her bike and needed a $2,000 surgery that her low-deductible insurance didn't cover. Now they found themselves unable to pay off the credit cards, which they had considered useful allies in an emergency and now realized that they were getting angry calls from creditors. It was five months into their new marriage and they were desperate, terrified, and hopeless because of their inability to pay for a combined $3,500 – half of what they made in a month – and the decision to buy a $24,000 truck...

So now you're budgeting, you are paying debt off aggressively, and you're making some side cash. None of this matters if the floor falls out from under you because of a sudden expense; more likely than not, you'll be understandably sucked into taking out debt, and you'll be taking three giant steps backwards[1]. Let's be clear: sudden emergencies happen to all of us and if you took out debt to pay for one, I can't begin to judge you – you were afraid and desperate. But having a fearless future is about lowering anxieties and giving yourself margin to make better choices[2]. So how do we keep the wolf away from the door without going into more debt – especially when we're focused on paying debt off?

— YOUR STARTER EMERGENCY FUND —

Before you do anything with your debt, I recommend scraping together as much extra money as you can spare – but no more than $2,000 – and place it in a "getting-out-of-debt" emergency fund[3]. You are never, ever, ever to touch this unless it is a genuine emergency (meaning, an unexpected, serious, and necessary cost), and even then I'd urge you to be slow to use it: see if you can do without the thing you are considering replacing, see if you can get it for cheap, or see if there is some alternative. Obviously, if a tire blows out, you need to replace it; if the fridge dies, it's got to be repaired; if a window breaks or a HVAC goes out in July or January, that needs tending. But be judicious about the cost until you have a full emergency fund.

You might wonder about the $2,000 and why it isn't lower or higher. In my estimation, this is just enough to handle a serious problem like a major appliance dying, but any more

---

[1] "9 Reasons You Need an Emergency Fund," *Kiplinger* (March 2012)
[2] "The True Cost of Debt," *The Simple Dollar* (December 2017)
[3] "How Much Should You Have in Your Emergency Fund?" *The Motley Fool*

than two grand is just money that you should be hurling at the debt[1]. And this shouldn't be your emergency fund for long: most people who aggressively go after debt pay it off in between six months and three years[2], so this is not a long-term solution – in fact, the idea is to make you nervous enough to motivate you[3]. So, for instance, if you have 20K in the bank right now, but you're 35K in debt, you need to pour $18,000 into your debt today. Yes, you'll feel nervous without that huge emergency fund, but how long does it take to pay off $17,000 if you're hustling? Probably six months to three years, depending on your income!

Let's say you have a $45,000 household income and $22,000 in student loans: you start your process in January, and have $2,000 in an emergency fund by Valentine's Day. Then you crank your income up to $50,000 by shoveling snow and walking dogs, you live on only $25,000, and you shovel the rest at the debt. By the next Valentine's Day you have it half-way done, which excites you enough to get a part time job, sending your income to $65,000. Still living on 25K – throwing $3,400 every month to debt – you are almost out of debt by September. Over the Fourth of July weekend, a neighbor shoots a pistol in the air and the bullet cracks your windshield (I don't know why your neighbors are categorically insane). The cost of the repair is $200. What do you do? You stop everything and refund your emergency fund before anything else. What if a bottle rocket caught some old leaves in your gutter on fire and your garage needs a repaired roof to the tune of $2,500? Pour cash on that repair like water on a fire: pay minimum payments on your debt until the repair its paid for, and do it with cash if possible.

— YOUR FULLY STOCKED MASTER EMERGENCY FUND —

---

[1] "How Much Should You Have in Your Emergency Fund?" *The Motley Fool*
[2] "The Dave Ramsey Baby Steps and Your Student Loan Debt," *The College Investor* (May 2018)
[3] "What If Your Emergency Fund Can't Cover Your Emergency?" *Dave Ramsey Blog*

By October you're debt free and you have so much momentum that – before you quit the part time job and stop walking dogs – you want to have a full emergency fund[1]. What should it look like? My wife and I needed two years to pay off our loans, and I was so relieved to start chucking money into this security net. Every paycheck that had been funneled to debt was now funneled to the emergency fund: we knew that when we were finished, we'd be able to replace the roof at the drop of a hat, buy a new heater if it went out in February, buy a used-but-safe car at a moment's notice, and repair a flooded basement at the blink of an eye. As a general rule, I recommend having an emergency fund that's roughly 3-6 months of general expenses – what it takes for you to live for a quarter-to-half of a year[2]. That's not what you *make* in 3-6 months, but what your *basic expenses* are (think the still-in-debt budget *minus* the debt payments). This doesn't mean a bare-bones, skeleton-crew monthly budget, but nor does it mean a fatty, indulgent, best-year-ever budget. Simply put: imagine you lost your job and were unemployed for four months (verrrrrrry unlikely if you have any work ethic or hustle, by the way, but just imagine) – what would you need?

Depending on your part of the country, your needs, your bills, and your lifestyle, this will be very different. Living in Fort Wayne, Indiana, the cost of living is very comfortable. Not as much in Brooklyn or Seattle. But for the sake of argument, let's use our original budget taken from a $72,000 income. It had room for utilities, rent, food, and clothing, as well as pets, haircuts, wellness, gas, giving, entertainment, and miscellaneous, and if you remove the 3 grand for debt, that leaves $3,000 for a fairly normal-if-thrifty lifestyle. In this case, I would recommend an emergency fund of between $9,000 and $18,000. Maybe you're making $32,000 and have very

---

[1] "Emergency Fund Calculator: How Much Will Protect You?" *Nerd Wallet* (October 2018)
[2] "How Much Should You Be Saving for an Emergency?" *Wells Fargo*

little wiggle room at all – a month's expenses for you might legitimately be $2,200. An emergency fund around $10,000 would be in order. If you'd feel more comfortable bumping that emergency fund up to six months, push that up to the full $13,200 – but I wouldn't advise you to have more than six months in your fund: to keep more money there would be robbing earning potential from your investments. And while we're on that topic remember: although it's possible to invest this and still keep it liquid, I do NOT recommend ever using your rainy day fund as an investment[1]. Don't put this in an IRA, or else you'll be taxed heavily when you take money out. Just keep this healthy, little emergency fund in the bank, only use it when you need it, and don't put more in – or take more out – than is necessary.

Ultimately, this is your lifeline to fearless finances: very few emergency expenses will fail to be met by this fund, and with it backing you up, you won't be terrified by a flat tire, freaked out by a dead battery, anxious about an unplanned tax payment, or put-off by an unexpected need to buy a plane ticket home. Dave Ramsey often quips that "an emergency fund turns a crisis into an inconvenience." That's exactly right: you'll be shocked at how easy-going and devil-may-care you are about inconveniences that would have made your life a living hell – you'll nonchalantly turn to your spouse and say "How much will the repair cost? Ugh. Whatever; take it out of the emergency fund." End of conversation. No desperate calls to parents, frantic searching for part time jobs, or freaked out eBay purges of used clothes, DVDs, and guitars. Nope: it'll be annoying, yes, inconvenient, yes, but a crisis, no.

---

[1] "Should You Invest Your Emergency Fund?" Nerd Wallet (February 2019)

PART TWO
— Paying Off Major Debts Fearlessly —

Credit card debt, vehicle debt, student loan debt,
And mortgages.

ଛ

CHAPTER 5.
— Credit Card and Consumer Debt —

"Your FICO score is not an indication of your success; all you've done is successfully paid payments and interest to the bank… Why are you giving banks money to run up a false measure of success?" – DAVE RAMSEY

"The rich rule over the poor, and the borrower is slave to the lender." – PROVERBS 22:7

Liam's dad taught him that it was critical to have a good credit score, so it was critical to have and use a credit card. "You can use it to pump gas or buy groceries. Just be sure to pay it off each month." Kaitlyn's mom used her credit card to medicate her depression, and since her parents never talked about money, and since they had a six-figure income, she assumed that credit cards were a source of happiness: if you wanted something, you could just buy it with credit and somehow it would get repaid – in time. So by October – after the A.C. broke, truck was wrecked, dental surgery was completed, and they had missed two credit payments – they tried opening another credit card to pay off the debt on the first. This seemed fine until Christmas, when they needed plane tickets back home to Ohio ($1,400) and almost $2,200 for Christmas gifts. The debt went on the second card, and they started paying it off in the New Year, but the day before Valentine's Day Kaitlyn's firm was sold and she lost her job. They went out to a sullen dinner at a high-end Alburquerque restaurant that night and quietly ate their lobster and chocolate cake. The bill was $149 without the tip. They put it on the credit card…

By now you won't be surprised to know that I don't have a very positive take on credit cards, but I understand if you or your partner do. Let's be honest: credit cards bring a feeling of security to many if not most people because it acts as an emergency fund – and I can't blame anyone for feeling warm towards the idea of having security[1]. That's the whole point of this book! In fact, I hope your emotions towards credit cards (if they're positive, that is) show you just how valuable security can be when it comes to finances. But the problem is that when someone lends you money, that means that until you have paid them back, they have power over you, and that should be terrifying[2]. For now it's just a few swipes here and there to pay for the gas or the groceries – all in order to build up a better credit score (a noble goal, right?), but if something should happen to the security net around you (a lost job, a car accident, a hospital visit, a sudden death requiring an unexpected trip back home...) then the ability to pay that debt back is suddenly cut off – and that's where the house of cards crumbles[3].

  So listen, I won't judge you if you have a credit card, but understand that it's dangerous anytime that you give someone else power over your finances. When I took the course to become a financial coach I paid for it in cash, and even though it made April's budget tight that year (we had to cancel a vacation in order to pay for the course outright), it was purchased and behind us. No better feeling, I promise you. It was done, and if it flopped or if it didn't work out, or if I changed my mind, I wasn't looking down the barrel of four months of installments – feeling like a failure each time the installment was due (or worse, be tight on cash one of those

---

[1] "Closing Credit Cards: What You Need to Know Right Now," www.jackiebeck.com (January 2019)
[2] "The True Cost of Debt," *The Simple Dollar* (December 2017)
[3] "Debt Horror Stories and Tales of Financial Woe," www.debt.com (October 2017)

months and not be able to pay a payment on a thing I wasn't doing anymore). Nope. Done and paid for!

So even though I know that many of you might disregard this advice, please consider ditching your credit cards: they need you, you don't need them. "What if I have an unexpected need?" Is it a *need* or a *want*? "This time it's a need." Okay, well then shuffle the budget and take it out of your gardening budget or your shopping or travel budget, or – if it's an emergency – out of the emergency fund. Say "no" to one thing so that you can say "yes" to this other thing. Do you *still* need it? Maybe not, or maybe you *do* need it and you're willing to give up eating out this month. Either way, it's your money, not some credit card company's, and YOU will always be a kinder lender to yourself than THEY are: you don't charge yourself interest, you don't call yourself in the middle of supper threatening to embarrass you at work or to harass your friends and family, and you don't need to explain your needs to yourself. Credit puts you under someone else's power and that almost always leads to fear[1]: what if they demand their payment now? What if they aren't generous or patient? What if they come for the car? The house?

— RUMPELSTILTSKIN AND THE "GOLD" CARD —

As an English professor I frequently taught the story of "Rumpelstiltskin" as a model story to break down and interpret, and so I'm going to tell it to you – straight from the Brothers' Grimm – and ask you what I asked my students: "what do you think this story is REALLY about...?"

There was once a miller who was poor, but he had one beautiful daughter. It happened one day that he came to speak with the king, and, to give himself consequence, he told him that he had a daughter who could spin gold out of straw. The king said to the miller: "That is an art that pleases me well; if thy daughter is as clever as you say, bring her to my castle to-morrow, that I may put her to the proof."

---

[1] "The Emotional Effects of Debt," *The Simple Dollar* (December 2017)

When the girl was brought to him, he led her into a room that was quite full of straw, and gave her a wheel and spindle, and said: "Now set to work, and if by the early morning thou hast not spun this straw to gold thou shalt die." And he shut the door himself, and left her there alone. And so the poor miller's daughter was left there sitting, and could not think what to do for her life: she had no notion how to set to work to spin gold from straw, and her distress grew so great that she began to weep. Then all at once the door opened, and in came a little man, who said: "Good evening, miller's daughter; why are you crying?"

"Oh!" answered the girl, "I have got to spin gold out of straw, and I don't understand the business." Then the little man said: "What will you give me if I spin it for you?" - "My necklace," said the girl. The little man took the necklace, seated himself before the wheel, and whirr, whirr, whirr! three times round and the bobbin was full; then he took up another, and whirr, whirr, whirr! three times round, and that was full; and so he went on till the morning, when all the straw had been spun, and all the bobbins were full of gold.

At sunrise came the king, and when he saw the gold he was astonished and very much rejoiced, for he was very avaricious. He had the miller's daughter taken into another room filled with straw, much bigger than the last, and told her that as she valued her life she must spin it all in one night. The girl did not know what to do, so she began to cry, and then the door opened, and the little man appeared and said: "What will you give me if I spin all this straw into gold?"

"The ring from my finger," answered the girl. So the little man took the ring, and began again to send the wheel whirring round, and by the next morning all the straw was spun into glistening gold. The king was rejoiced beyond measure at the sight, but as he could never have enough of gold, he had the miller's daughter taken into a still larger room full of straw, and said: "This, too, must be spun in one night, and if you accomplish it you shall be my wife." For he thought: "Although she is but a miller's daughter, I am not likely to find any one richer in the whole world." As soon as the girl was left alone, the little man appeared for the third time and said: "What will you give me if I spin the straw for you this time?" - "I have nothing left to give," answered the girl. "Then you must promise me the first child you have after you are queen," said the little man. "But who knows whether that will happen?" thought the girl; but as she did not know what else to do in her necessity, she promised the little man what he desired, upon which he began to spin, until all the straw was gold. And when in the morning the king came and found all done according to his wish, he caused the wedding to be held at once, and the miller's pretty daughter became a queen.

In a year's time she brought a fine child into the world, and thought no more of the little man; but one day he came suddenly into her room, and said: "Now give me what you promised me." The queen was terrified greatly, and offered the little man all the riches of the kingdom if he would only leave the child; but the little man said: "No, I would rather have something living than all the treasures of the world." Then the queen began to lament and to weep, so that the little man had pity upon her. "I will give you three days," said he, "and if at the end of that time you cannot tell my name, you must give up the child to me."

Then the queen spent the whole night in thinking over all the names that she had ever heard, and sent a messenger through the land to ask far and wide for all the names that could be found. And when the little man came next day, (beginning with Caspar, Melchior, Balthazar) she repeated all she knew, and went through the whole list, but after each the little man said: "That is not my name." The second day the queen sent to inquire of all the neighbours what the servants were called, and told the little man all the most unusual and singular names, saying: "Perhaps you are called Roast-ribs, or Sheepshanks, or Spindleshanks?" But he answered nothing but: "That is not my name."

The third day the messenger came back again, and said: "I have not been able to find one single new name; but as I passed through the woods I came to a high hill, and near it was a little house, and before the house burned a fire, and round the fire danced a comical little man, and he hopped on one leg and cried:

"Today do I bake,
tomorrow I brew,
The day after that the queen's child comes in;
And oh! I am glad that nobody knew
That the name I am called is Rumpelstiltskin!"

You cannot think how pleased the queen was to hear that name, and soon afterwards, when the little man walked in and said: "Now, Mrs. Queen, what is my name?" she said at first "Are you called Jack?" - "No," answered he. "Are you called Harry?" she asked again. "No," answered he. And then she said": "Then perhaps your name is Rumpelstiltskin?"

"The devil told you that! the devil told you that!" cried the little man, and in his anger he stamped with his right foot so hard that it went into the ground above his knee; then he seized his left foot with both his hands in such a fury that he split in two, and there was an end of him…

So what do you think? She begs for help and at first he seems so kind and helpful, but when he comes back to collect, all the kindness is gone: she owes him her child's life (the future happiness and security of her family), but to him it's just business. Now, there are tons of ways to read this old, German tale, but at its heart it's a cautionary tale about being careful with creditors[1]. At first they seem like fast friends, but deny them their due and they turn against you.

---

[1] "The Sociocultural Feminist Implications of 'Rumpelstiltskin'," Emily Barsic, Emma Hartman, and Alexis Lawhorn, Ball State University (2015)

So if you're paying off credit cards, here's my advice: do it fast and be aggressive. Pile on money frantically and get it out of your life. You don't need credit if you plan to fund your own life through your own efforts – to say no to impulse and build a life of peace and confidence[1]. Yes, most people do eventually take out mortgages or student loans, but credit cards are different – these are choices to purchase toys you can't afford, and while I'm absolutely positive that most people with credit cards have used them to buy something they actually did desperately need (a replacement tire, a broken furnace, a surgery for a beloved pet), I'd love to see you get to a point where you have an emergency fund that can replace creditors[2]. I'm not upset at you if you're using a credit card now, but please wean yourself off of it and become your own credit card company to yourself – trust me, you'll be the kindest lender in the world!

---

[1] "You Don't Need a Credit Score, Here's an Alternative," www.cfinancialfreedom.com (September 2012)
[2] "Why It's Not Ideal to Use a Credit Card for Emergencies," *The Balance* (January 2019)

CHAPTER 6.
— Vehicle Loans and Car Leases —

"The second you drive that car off the lot, it depreciates, 10%, 20%... Let somebody else get that depreciation... Most people I know who are really wealthy, they keep their cars five, ten years." – SUZE ORMAN

"A man without self-control is like a city broken into and left without walls." – PROVERBS 25:28

Faced now with a 40K income and over 60K in debt – 12K in credit cards, 24K on Liam's new truck, and the rest in student loans – Kaitlyn felt herself becoming severely depressed – like her mother had been growing up. But she had begun to sense that credit cards wouldn't ease the anxiety. She found a part time job at Target and started researching getting out of debt. What she read horrified her – she realized how foolish they had been with their finances – but gave her hope. She talked to Liam about it, and his face grew ashen. He realized, without her saying anything, that the quickest way to ease their debt would be to sell his truck. It had gone down in value some, but would easily be able to knock out their consumer debt and take a bite out of their student loans. She let him consider it for a week, and by springtime he was driving a twelve year old Honda with rust and scratches, but he quietly smiled to himself whenever he saw it or thought about how hopeful Kaitlyn was now: it was the first grownup sacrifice he had ever made, and he felt ten times the man riding in that bouncy Honda than he had in his new truck...

༄

Let's talk cars. Cars are usually the second biggest purchase that Americans make in their lifetimes, second to houses, and for renters, they're the biggest purchase only rivalled by student loans[1]. Cars are status symbols to lots of folks, and a new car is something that most people aspire to have at some point in their life – if not every few years (...if not every year!). But how do cars stack up as an investment compared to houses and student loans? In a word... poorly. Houses, barring sudden shifts in demographics, industries, or natural disasters go up in value at a mathematically significant rate. My own house is in a modest, blue-collar, middle-class, urban neighborhood, and it's gone up about 20% in the four years since we bought it. Student loans – assuming you didn't major in interpretive dance, general studies, or medieval French drama – should repay themselves in a few years if you pay them off aggressively, and your education should become the source of almost every dollar you make. Cars, on the other hand, plummet in value as soon as they leave the dealership, and decline in value every year[2]. Everything with an engine does this – even classic cars and collectibles[3]. This makes a car a terrible place to invest money, but a necessary purchase for most folks who don't live in New York or London.

So what should you do, then? Short answer: make that purchase a reasonable percentage of your income, because whatever you invest in it won't be coming back. My rule of thumb is no more than 30%[4] of your household income (a $9,000 car for a $30,000 income; $18,000 for a $60,000 house; $27,000 for a $60,000 family). There's nothing wrong with a nice car or even a new one as long as it's a sensible percentage of your pay, but when it begins to creep up on your disposable income – swallowing more than a car should

---

[1] "Five Expenses that will Consume 50% of your Lifetime Income," *Forbes* (August 2010)
[2] "Self-Made Millionaire: 'Buying a New Car is the Single Worst Financial Decision," *CNBC Money* (October 2018)
[3] "Has the Collector Car Market Bubble Burst?" *BestRide.com* (October 2017)
[4] "Five Expenses that will Consume 50% of your Lifetime Income," *Forbes* (August 2010)

merit – it starts to hold back your potential: instead of investing in your future, giving generously to others, or being able to afford a spontaneous weekend trip, your money is beholden to the rolling, metal box in your garage.

So, a quick question: are cars – said rolling, metal boxes – worth taking a lease out on? ABSOLUTELY NOT! Instead of taking out a disastrous, high-interest, predatory[1] lease on a silly car, acknowledge that it is only a contraption used to move you around (not an extension of your worth, value, or identity as a human being) and simply buy a car you can afford. If you do have a lease, try to get out of it: beg, plead, offer them money, and never go into one again. Most people accept the fact that leasing a car is a terrible choice, but if you're on the fence, please take my advice and avoid it at all costs: as ruthless and predatory as a payday lender, car leases are wealth killers that you should never consider[2].

Personally, I'll never even recommend a car loan, but I understand that most people will ignore this advice, so if you must get a car loan, make it something you can pay off very quickly. Don't be the guy with a $34,000 income and a $36,000 car. *Never be that guy*. But I will again urge you to save up for a car that you can afford and buy it with cash: let's say you have a $9,000 car and want a $15,000 replacement – be intentional by setting aside a grand or so each month for six months, sell the old car, save that cash, and put the two piles together. If, however, you already have a car loan, follow the same process to get out of debt detailed in Part One, even if it means dumping all but $2,000 from your emergency fund. Ideally, this wouldn't happen because you would plan ahead, save up, and buy the car with cash, but if you are in a bind, then go back to the beginning, use the emergency fund's reserves, and then start over (never intentionally use the emergency fund to buy a car, though – it's only for emergencies and for getting out of debt).

---

[1] "Suze Orman: 'Don't Ever Lease a Car," *CNBC Money* (September 2018)
[2] "Leasing Creates the Illusion, Not Reality, of Wealth," *Interest.com* (August 2015)

CHAPTER 7.
— Student Loans —

"For-profit higher education is today a booming industry, feeding on the student loans handed out to the desperate."
– THOMAS FRANK

"Do not be one who shakes hands in pledge or puts up security for debts; if you lack the means to pay, your very bed will be snatched from under you." – PROVERBS 22:26-27

Carleigh was accepted to a private four year college in 2008 and graduated with a double major in history and psychology in 2012 with $122,000 in student loans. She wasn't worried until her last semester when, for the first time it seemed, she began to wonder what she would do with the degrees. She had been swept up by the intellectual atmosphere, the friendships, the sorority house, the feeling of being part of something bigger than yourself – a 200 year old college in a beautiful city hundreds of miles from her Missouri hometown – and the limitless possibilities that her professors constantly preached about. Knowledge, they explained, was priceless, and college was the place to go if you wanted to be fully human. She began to cringe at the thought of graduation, and talked to some professors about going onto grad school, where her loans would be deferred and should continue her intellectual evolution. And so, in August, she went to another private school and started her master's degree in English. Two years later she finally had to pause the momentum and ask "what was all of this for?" She had added twenty grand to her pricetag, and had to decide whether she was going to tack on more for a PhD – just to delay the inevitable. She decided that four more years of *school – which would probably result in an adjunct professor's job of $18,000 - $24,000, at least for the first four years – wasn't a good plan. So she left the academic world and found herself almost 150K in debt and working two part time jobs at her hometown's history center and a Texas Roadhouse restaurant. The combined salary of $32,000 was enough to start chipping away at the debt, but she was 27 and living at home, using a bike for transportation, and still unsure of who had told her that six years of higher education was priceless. She knew the price tag…*

∞

America's student debt crisis has passed the 1.5 trillion mark, leaving tens of millions of young people and back-to-school-adults in desperation and fear[1]. When I was eighteen, in 2006, I was lead to believe that a college education was a flawless investment: you got out what you spent. This meant that private schools were a good place to go to college whether you had the money or not, and that employers would pay more for a more uppity education. I was halfway through college when the financial crisis hit, and I left my private university with $30,000 in debt for an English major. How is it possible that I realize I was one of the luckier ones? Other classmates of mine were stuck with 150K for a history degree (now working at a genealogy center), 120K for a philosophy degree (giving guitar lessons and bartending), and over 150K for a public relations major and master's in theology (manager at a Texas Roadhouse). Please avoid this kind of insanity by only taking on the education you can afford and by rejecting some common assumptions about what you or your children are entitled to.

  Firstly, we pay off student debt like any other, but the way we avoid it is unique: there are several steps you can take to be wisely educated. Most important of these is school

---

[1] "Student Loan Debt Statistics in 2019: A $1.5 Trillion Crisis," *Forbes* (February 2019)

choice: you can go to any school you can afford, but if you can't pay in cash, consider going to an in-state, public university (average cost of a resident is $9,900, or $190 a week[1] – which a student can cash flow by waiting tables, walking dogs, or giving music lessons). Living costs are another $12,000 a year on average, so a student might choose to live at home and commute. In fact, one really good idea for saving on college money is going to a community college for two years (average tuition: a staggeringly palatable $4,800[2], sometimes as low as $1,600), scooping up the prerequisites, and then transferring to a four-year school for your last two years. The degree will say Purdue or Ohio State or USC regardless of where you spent the first two years. Even if you decide that they need to live in the dorms (which I wouldn't call a "need" – more maturity and "life-lessons" can be learned through paying your way through college with work and grit and determination than by living in a dorm and playing beer pong), this is only about 24K a year, and if the student is working a part time job (which they should), scholarships can be part of your plan to take up the slack after $15K - $20K come in from work. www.MyScholly.com is a great website to scan for scholarships, and if the student submits just one scholarship a day as they head towards college – even if they get only 5% of their submissions accepted – that's hundreds of dollars of potential which can mean free books or even a free semester[3].

    Also, be careful of what you study: pick a major with marketable potential that intersects with your interests and skills. That means very creative types shouldn't get accounting degrees *just* because they pay well, but nor should they major in interpretive dance or anthropology: try marketing, psychology, architecture, interior design, or

---

[1] "Average Cost of College in America: 2019 Report," *ValuePenguin*, (2019)
[2] "Average Community College Tuition Costs," *Community College Review* (2019)
[3] "How Much Can a Student Win from Scholarships?" *Investopedia* (October 2018)

graphic design, instead. I majored in English and while life has worked out for me very well, it's mostly because my wife, a hard-working social worker, has killed it in her profession, and because I've been lucky to rise up the ranks. The humanities are beautiful and sublime – but you can learn about them by auditing a class, checking books out of the library, or watching documentaries on Netflix. Your major and your interests are two different things: a major is a course of study designed to build a profitable career. This is why an engineer may love playing guitar but not have majored in guitar performance, or why a chemistry teacher may love painting, but didn't major in creative arts, or why a therapist may love the poems of Dante and Goethe, but didn't major in Italian Renaissance Literature or Romantic German Poetry. You can have a passion or hobby that builds your soul – but don't waste your four years of college earning an expensive degree that employers aren't hiring for.

    Folks interested in grad school will likewise find that attending a local, public college is far wiser than shelling out four times as much just for a prettier campus or a fancier sounding education. I've never, ever asked anyone I've paid for work where they went to college: doctors, nurses, dentists, mechanics, bankers, therapists, CPA's, none of 'em. And I doubt you have either – no one really does unless their just conversing or being friendly. All that matters is that they have a degree from somewhere[1]. Folks planning on being doctors or lawyers or something similarly expensive are probably unlikely to get out of grad school without debt, but even they can be smart about how expensive their school is, how many scholarships they apply for, and how hard they work to make extra income. After graduation, doctors and lawyers who still live like students for two or three years will avoid the expensive extravagances of their peers, be able to save up

---

[1] "Back Off: It Doesn't Matter What College Your Kids Attend," *Psychology Today* (Dec 2019)

piles of cash, and be able to use their impressive incomes to blow the debt out in three years or less.

In short, be very careful about what you use your education for. Some people see college as a mandatory rite of passage and excuse blowing 100K on a French drama degree or a double major in dance and feminist dialectics, and are then deeply hurt and jaded when they are working at a college-town vegan coffee shop five years later, paying minimum payments and venting their rage at the employer's Friday night smash poetry contests. Besides which, vegan coffee shops rarely have 401Ks or good dental plans.

CHAPTER 8.
— Real Estate and Mortgages —

"If you can afford to purchase a home within your budget, it's a good decision to buy. But wrecking your budget just to own a house makes no sense at all. The compulsion Americans have for buying large, expensive homes is just a reflection of poor stewardship…" – LARRY BURKETT

"The wise woman builds her house, but with her own hands the foolish one tears hers down." – PROVERBS 14:1

Jackson and Blakely had a toddler and an infant and felt that it was time to move out of their two bedroom apartment and find a house to settle into. Their growing family needed a lot: a finished basement, a house less than twenty years old, four bathrooms, four bedrooms (one for each child, plus a guest room for weekend visitors), an open floorplan, a backyard with a fence, a gated community, a two-car garage, a playground, room for a hot tub, and a solid school system. The graphic designer and photographer made a total of $74,000 a year, and found that the houses closest to their dream home were all the neighborhood of $290,000. Jackson started to wonder if they could really afford the estimated $2,332 monthly mortgage payments, but Blakely was resolved: their children needed to have a safe place to live (which also required separate bedrooms, a two car garage, etc.), and so they bought a home that came relatively close to their ideal. With almost 40% of their income going towards the mortgage however – and the realization that their 14 year old house was quickly and cheaply built, with a leaking basement, rotting roof, and cheap water heater – they started to feel like their dream was slowly drifting into a nightmare…

It's been part of the American dream for centuries, but in 2008, it caused the greatest crisis in American financial confidence and anxiety since 1929[1]. Homeownership is a noble and worthy goal, and its financial benefits are multifaceted: although houses have recently been outranked by stocks and mutual funds in most Americans' investment portfolios, the confidence and self-worth that homeownership can bring to a family is not to be sneezed at[2]. But not everyone is financially ready to shoulder a mortgage: the 2008 crash happened because banks were giving houses to people who couldn't afford them[3], and the results were cataclysmic. So who can afford a house, when do you know you should buy, and what should you buy?

  There are four tips I have for homebuyers. Firstly, I recommend that folks looking for real estate limit themselves to **fixed-rate mortgages**: the interest will not rise and fall depending on the economy, but stay fixed at the rate available at the time you purchase it; this can be refinanced at another time if the interest rates become more affordable. Secondly, I highly, highly encourage you to find a **15 year mortgage** (if you already have a 30 year mortgage, try paying it off LIKE a fifteen year by doubling your payments – never refinance to a fifteen), because this ensures that you can afford the payments, and that you'll own your equity in a relatively short period of time. It's often been said before that 100% of foreclosures have mortgages on them: the sooner your mortgages is paid off, the better you'll sleep at night!

  Thirdly, I would suggest that you be able to put **10% down** (if you can swing 20% -- which most can't – that would be even better because you'll avoid requiring **Private Mortgage Insurance**). I know this is a pretty staggering suggestion for most people, but please consider saving up for

---

[1] "Market Crashes: Housing Bubble and Credit Crisis (2007 – 2008)," *Investopedia* (2018)
[2] "Real Estate No Longer Top Investment Choice for Americans," *Housing Wire* (July 2018)
[3] "Recession: CNBC Explains," *CNBC Money* (July 2011)

a year or so and being able to plop that $15,000 down for a 150K house; don't be impatient, because there'll always be houses for sale, even if you need to wait a little while longer. Lastly, I recommend being very wise and intentional about where you buy a house. Pick a **neighborhood with stability**: ask realtors what the average days on the market are for houses in the neighborhood you're checking out, and don't linger in places where it takes over a month to sell. It's all right to buy in a modest, humble, blue-collar neighborhood – I live in one and my house has gone up tens of thousands of dollars in just four years – but be careful about settling in a place where the houses have boarded windows, high weeds, and rusting cars – where the liquor stores outnumber the pharmacies and which the evening news seems to feature a bit too much for crime. These areas need love and compassion, but you should be careful about taking up a mortgage there. If you buy in a healthy neighborhood with a rising market, you should be able to anticipate steady gains in your equity over the years – even if it dips down from time to time (all neighborhoods do).

Lastly, let me recommend another great online tool: the **Dave Ramsey Mortgage Calculator** (just Google it). It uses the first three metrics I listed to determine what kind of house you can afford and helps you to avoid the emotional and financial terror of a foreclosure. For example, I typed in a house worth $200,000, included a down payment of 10%, and figured 15-year-fixed with an interest rate of 3.6%. The breakdown of costs would be a monthly cost (including insurance, property taxes, PMI, and the mortgage) of $1,624 – which is totally doable for some families and kind of hefty for others. Or say we looked at a $120,000 house with 10% down, 15- fixed, with 4.0% in interest. That changes the cost to $962.

Check this calculator out and play around with it to figure out what kind of house you can afford, and then resist the urge to repeat the Great Recession and only buy a home that you can reasonably pay off in fifteen years.

PART THREE
— Preparing for a Fearless Future —

Understanding and getting a nest egg,
Insurance, and a will.

CHAPTER 9.
— Understanding & Getting a Nest Egg —

"It's not how much money you make, but how much money you keep, how hard it works for you, and how many generations you keep it for." – ROBERT KIYOSAKI

"Put your investments in several places – many places even – because you never know what kind of bad luck you are going to have in this world." – ECCLESIATES 11:2

Ben and Alyssa were both 27 and had been married for two years when they found out that they were pregnant. Before this, they hadn't ever really thought about the future, but Ben's dad suggested they should look into investing in more than just their works' Vanguard 401K's. They supposed they could potentially put aside a quarter of a million if they were heavily investing, but his dad urged them to check out Chris Hogan's R:IQ Calculator online and see what it tabulated. They had a modest, Midwestern income of $64,000, and decided that their goals were mostly spending time with family – camping, playing games, doing road trips – and that their monthly expenses were probably around $5,330. Presuming retirement at the age of 65, they adjusted the calculator and hit "enter." They were shocked: by investing just $324 a month they could expect to yield almost $3,000,000 in a nest egg. That didn't even factor in their future raises or promotions, and even if the interest rate fluctuated, they – an art teacher and a youth pastor – would be millionaires by their early fifties if they started now...

೫ఎ

Retirement isn't something that most young people think about, but I've noticed that more and more are. People are watching their parents and grandparents face retirement with fear and it's scaring them[1]. The key to a fearless future is having a plan for retirement, and that means understanding what your goals are. My wife and I are very simple people – homebodies who enjoy gardening, house projects, and staying in on Friday nights. Our goal for retirement is to take it easy and enjoy our nest, but many – if not most – people have loftier ambitions: more travel, longer vacations, bigger houses, nicer cars, warmer climates. Others have hobbies they want to invest more money in, second careers they want to start, or families they want to visit on the regular. It's almost impossible to envision this kind of a life without a solid retirement in mind: social security hardly pays enough to keep folks' lights and water on, and if you let your company manage your portfolio for you, you can't be sure that you're getting the energetic-but-conservative 10%+ return that you can be getting from wisely invested Roth IRA's[2]. If you want to avoid a future of anxiety and uncertainty, the first thing to do is to determine what your retirement looks like in your mind's eye.

    The best tool for this is **Chris Hogan's Retirement IQ Calculator** at www.chrishogan360.com/riq/. This is a fantastic, free service that leads you through the mathematics of figuring out how much you should be investing in solid IRA's depending on your means, goals, and timeline. It's never too early or too late to start. If you go to this site you'll be asked to enter your email (they don't bomb you with emails, but if you don't enjoy the content – which I personally love – you can always unsubscribe) and will be led to a screen with six options asking you which best represents your dream

---

[1] "Wait, What? Millennials Better Prepared for Retirement than Parents," *401k Specialist Mag* (May 2018)
[2] "How to Make 12% Annually... Forever," *Forbes* (January 2017)

retirement: Relaxation, Family, Hobbies, Recreation, Travel, or Other. Let's say you're into Travel. Okay, now you're led to a screen asking for your household income (it's a secure site, so you can feel comfortable punching it in). Let's say $70,000. You are then taken to a sliding bar where you can adjust your monthly needs between MODEST and EXTRAVAGANT. The mean of $70,000 is $5,834, but let's say you're a little bit high maintenance and slide the scale towards EXTRAVAGANT to the tune of $7,800 a month. Now you're asked how long it will be before your retirement. Hmm... Say, 30 years. Now the calculator asks how much you have saved already. Perhaps you're just starting today, so we'll say $0.

    To lead this lifestyle, you need to save $3.5 million in retirement, and to do this, you need to be investing $1,000 a month in retirement. How does that stack with my recommended investment of 15%? It's a little more aggressive: $1,000/month on a 70K salary is 17% of your income, but how much more do you need to earn to make that only 15%? $10,000 a year – or about $200 a month. Perhaps you feel like you could live on less than that $7,800 a month if it means not needing the extra cash: if you changed it to $6,000/month then the recommended monthly investment is only $775, or 13% of your income. Crank that up to fifteen and you're looking at a nest egg of over $3 million! And that's still with zero savings as of yet and a retirement ideal that might realistically cool down as you age (right now you might want to spend three weeks in Europe every summer, but at 65 you might decide that one week every other year is pretty good, too).

    Now when it comes to investments, there are several tools that you'll have to choose from: your work's retirement plan or pension, single stocks and bonds, Roth IRA's, certificates of deposit, fixed or variable annuities, whole life insurance, precious metals, real estate, and exchange traded funds. There's only three of those that I would even consider: the rest work hard for other people sell you short. First I'll explain the instruments that I don't recommend, then

I'll explain the three systems that I'd suggest you use, and lastly, I'll teach you how to use those three systems to the best of their capacity.

— INVESTMENT SYSTEMS TO AVOID —

— SINGLE STOCKS —

What it is: Stock in public businesses like Apple, Lowes, Target, Dairy Queen, Coca-Cola, and Dollar General[1]. Instead of investing in a pool of stocks (a mutual fund), this approach places the entire investment in one basket, where it will rise and fall with that company's fortunes and misfortunes.

Why you should avoid it: This is obviously a bad idea because even widely lauded titans of the stock market can crash (this happened when the dotcom bubble burst in the early 2000's and when the housing market crashed in the late 2000's)[2]. You might think nothing could ever topple Apple, Disney, or McDonald's – but never say never. As so many people learned when their company stock was obliterated in 2008 – causing a rash of suicides, divorces, and poverty – you should never have all your eggs in one basket.

— BONDS —

What it is: These are fixed income investments which pay the owner for the loan of money to a borrower like a government or a business[3]. For example, treasury bonds are sold by the U.S. government, which will return the money lent to it with a modest return. Bonds are popular because they are considered a safe investment (they'll be returned as long as the U.S. government, for example, is in place, which is a more

---

[1] "Stock," *Investopedia* (March 2019)
[2] "Stock," *Investopedia* (March 2019)
[3] "Bond," *Investopedia* (February 2019)

trustworthy investment than a start-up microbrewery in a bad neighborhood, for example). Bonds are basically I.O.U.'s sold by large entities to grow their projects and are often connected to a specific project (military defense, paving roads, opening a second bank branch, etc.). The bond comes with a specific end date upon which the borrower must be paid back with interest, and may be fixed or variable.

Why you should avoid it: Polar opposites of single stocks in one sense, bonds are conservative to a fault – they're certainly trustworthy and dependable, but provide weak, anemic returns[1]. You'll get money back from them, but only at a drip.

— CERTIFICATES OF DEPOSIT —

What it is: These are savings certificates that feature a fixed date of maturity (or date of withdrawal) and a fixed interest rate[2]. Federally insured, they don't have monthly fees, and are secure investments, but unlike a typical savings account (and akin to an annuity) you are unable to access these funds without paying a penalty during the term of investment (which can range from days to a decade). Although they tend to have fixed interest rates, the longer the term is, the higher the rate will be.

Why you should avoid it: CD's introduce some of the recurring problems of clunky investment tools: they have limited liquidity (you can't easily access your money if needs arise), they lag behind inflation, cancelling out the benefits of their interest rates, and their returns – like those of bonds – are unimpressive[3]. Nowhere near as volatile or stupid as single stocks or cryptocurrency, but their lack of energy makes them a wasteful investment.

---

[1] "Bond," *Investopedia* (February 2019)
[2] "Certificate of Deposit," *Investopedia* (November 2018)
[3] "Certificate of Deposit," *Investopedia* (November 2018)

— FIXED ANNUITIES —

What it is: An annuity is a long term investment which pays the holder an annual amount[1]. Financial advisors who sell annuities (which are a fairly expensive investment, requiring an average of 3%-4% in cost – not interest FOR you, but interest due FROM you). Annuities suggest that they are risk-averse because they required long-term investing to participate, which prevents people from pulling out when the market bucks. Fixed rate annuities have a guaranteed rate of return that protects you from slumps but doesn't offer the higher paybacks that variable annuities promise to offer during peaks.

Why you should avoid it: People are drawn to annuities because of the annual returns and their perceived imperviousness to the market. However, if the market does ever tank, this will drag annuities down the tubes with them, so while they aren't as volatile as single stocks, they're on the same footing as any other mainstream investment[2]. And then there are the more glaring issues: they are simultaneously expensive (they come with administration charges, mortality fees, and expense costs that nickel-and-dime investors) and anemic (lagging behind the stock market like bonds). They are also almost impossible to exit, and your money cannot be removed from the annuity to benefit your heirs. Ultimately, their expense (often costing as much as 50% of the value), rigidity, and poor returns combine to make this a mostly bad investment.

— VARIABLE ANNUITIES —

What it is: Like fixed annuities, these are long-term investments which are stuck in place, require you to pay for them, and

---

[1] "Fixed Annuity," *Investopedia* (March 2018)
[2] "Fixed Annuity," *Investopedia* (March 2018)

shell out a yearly payment[1]. Unlike fixed rate annuities, variables are dynamic and bend and flex with the market, meaning you'll gain more during a bull market, and lose more during a bear market.

Why you should avoid it: Same concerns as fixed annuities, except that these are also volatile and jumpy, bringing pleasantly high highs, but vulnerable to the market's careening lows[2]. Hard pass.

— WHOLE LIFE INSURANCE —

What it is: Whole life policies are complicated instruments that attempt to do several things: act as an investment, act as insurance, and act as a savings account. Their premiums are about 3-5 times more expensive than a term policy, and generally make less than 2% in returns[3]. However, its selling point is that you are able to build up a "cash value" over time by steadily investing in it. Upon the policy holder's death, the total cash value of the policy is given to their heirs. Another supposed benefit is that the premiums are high but stay the same, while term policies go up as you age.

Why you should avoid it: This one is such a tangled mess that I'm going to let Dave Ramsey himself explain the Wild West landscape of its empty promises[4]: "Let's say a 30-year-old man has $100 per month to spend on life insurance. He shops around and finds he can purchase an average of $125,000 in insurance for his family. From the whole life insurance agent, he'll probably hear a pitch for a $100 per month policy that will build up savings for retirement, which is what a cash value policy is supposed to do. However, if he purchases 20-year term life insurance with coverage of $125,000, it will cost him only about $7 per month instead of $100.

---

[1] "Variable Annuity," *Investopedia* (March 2018)
[2] "Variable Annuity," *Investopedia* (March 2018)
[3] "Whole Life Insurance," *Investopedia* (April 2018)
[4] "Term Life vs. Whole Life Insurance," *Dave Ramsey Blog* (2018)

"So, if he goes with the cash value option, the other $93 per month should be added to his whole life insurance payout amount, right? Well, not really. You see, there are expenses . . .

"All of the $93 per month disappears into commissions and expenses for the first three years. After that, the cash value portion of his policy will average a 1.5% return per year for a whole life guaranteed cash value policy according to Consumer Reports.

"Worse yet, the savings he does manage to build up after being ripped off for years won't even go to his family when he passes away! The only benefit his family will receive is the face value of the policy, which was $125,000 in our example.

"But what if he invested that $93 each month for 20 years? With a 10% rate of return, that would turn into about $70,000. Even better, if he invested for 30 years it would turn into over $200,000! Talk about a lot of bang for your buck!"

— PRECIOUS METALS —

What it is: Out of an unfounded fear that the global economy could self-destruct, leaving fiat currency defunct, many people have used gold or silver or jewelry as a physical investment to protect them in case of an economic cataclysm: if no one accepts credit cards or debit cards or honors printed money, surely you can trade gold coins for gas and bottled water, right[1]?

Why you should avoid it: If the economy collapses, people actually used goods – like gas and bottled water – as currency, not shiny rocks or inedible doubloons[2]. History has vouched for this: in the aftermath of economic collapses (e.g., Germany after the World Wars), recovering populations

---

[1] "28 Reasons to Buy Physical Gold," *Bullion Star* (November 2017)
[2] "Why Gold Would be Useless in an Economic Apocalypse," *The Atlantic* (December 2013)

dispensed with cash or coins and began trading usable assets like chickens, wheat, coats, bottles, and lamp oil for goods they needed. If the economy crashes, your gold will be worthless, while the hipster with a chicken coop in his backyard and a homemade pickle business will become an apocalyptic tycoon[1]. Also, be aware that precious metals have a terrible history of returns[2]: they skyrocket when the market sags, but then return to where they began – they are tantamount to investing $10,000 at 1.5% and expecting to become a millionaire.

— CRYPTO-CURRENCIES —

What it is: A hot and trendy investment tool, crypto-currencies like Bitcoin attract attention because they promise to be the new Apple (proverbially, everyone wishes they had invested in Apple or Microsoft stock in the mid-80's)[3]. Basically digital money backed by what are called "strong cryptos," this decentralized form of money is traded online and used in the same way that most people use dollars, pounds, or yen[4].
Why you should avoid it: Maybe it will be a great success – and most economic minds think that it has a future[5] (though they are in disagreement as to how brilliant it will be) – but it's not worth risking your nest egg on a hot new trend (again, see: dotcom bubble, housing bubble, et al.), and many theorists believe that a cryptocurrency bubble is building which will eventually ruin the hopes of people who have poured their money into it[6]. If you buy cryptocurrency, be

---

[1] "Gold or Silver Won't Do Much Good in an Economic Collapse," *Seattle Times* (August 2016)
[2] "Four Reasons why Gold is a Bad Investment," *Forbes* (November 2018)
[3] "Should You Invest in Bitcoin? 10 Arguments in Favor as of December 2015," *Forbes* (December 2015)
[4] "Cryptocurrency," *Investopedia* (February 2019)
[5] "The Role of Cryptocurrency in a Future Society," *Forbes* (October 2018)
[6] "Warren Buffet and Jamie Dimon on Bitcoin: Beware," *CNBC Markets* (June 2018)

sure that you spend no more than 2% of your income on it. See how it does over five years, and then we'll talk...

— EXCHANGE TRADED FUNDS —

What it is: This is a marketable security which is tied to a stock index – similar to a mutual fund[1]. However, unlike mutual funds, ETF shares are traded like common stock on the exchanges, causing their prices to fluctuate more unpredictably and to invite both excitement and anxiety.
Why you should avoid it: Although ETF's are more liquid and less volatile than many of the systems on this list, it still comes up short[2]. They still can nickel-and-dime you with commissions and fees, lack the spectrum of diversity that I would recommend for secure-yet-profitable investing, and can be tied to untested indices, which increase risk and cancel out some of the benefits. Overall, this is better than most, but still fails to match the security and profitability of the wider market.

— REAL ESTATE INVESTMENT TRUST —

What it is: This permits individual investors to buy shares of various real estate portfolios through commercial organizations[3]. This includes things like warehouses, office buildings, apartments, retail space, healthcare facilities, infrastructure, and land used for farming, timber, or mining.
Why you should avoid it: REIT's are easy to trade, but their dividends are heavily regulated and are taxed as ordinary income[4]. This fact alone makes them pale in comparison to tax-sheltered Roth IRA's, and while they – like bonds – are usually stable, conservative, and reliable, they yield notably thin returns after taxes are taken out.

---

[1] "Exchange Traded Fund," *Investopedia* (January 2019)
[2] "Exchange Traded Fund," *Investopedia* (January 2019)
[3] "Real Estate Investment Trust," *Investopedia* (November 2018)
[4] "Real Estate Investment Trust," *Investopedia* (November 2018)

— SEPARATE ACCOUNT MANAGERS —

What it is: This is a portfolio of individual securities which are fostered by a management firm on your behalf[1]. You are given ownership of the individual securities, which claim to provide you with control while the firm monitors its progress.
Why you should avoid it: The main difference between SMA's and IRA's is that each portfolio is unique to a single account rather than being lumped in with other investors, which allows for more choice and freedom[2]. However, with this comes risk: by floating off to sea in search of different fish, it stands to run into sharks. While SMA's are a relatively stable option, their potential volatility outweighs the perks.

— YOUR WORK PENSION —

What is it: Rarer and rarer now that 401K's are universal, pensions are retirement plans made available to a worker after retirement[3]. The longer they serve a company, the more they are due, and upon retirement, this is usually doled out in installments like a downsized paycheck.
Why you should avoid it: Well... not *avoid it per se* (take it if it's offered), but NEVER depend on it. If a company tanks, its pensions often tank, too. Most people don't realize this. 401K's, however, are not connected to a particular workplace, and are a much better option because, even if the business closes up shop, a 401K will still be available. Pensions, however, go down with the ship[4].

---

[1] "Separate Account," *Investopedia* (April 2018)
[2] "Separate Account," *Investopedia* (April 2018)
[3] "Pension Plan," *Investopedia* (February 2019)
[4] "Don't Count on Pension Plans for Your Retirement," *Newsmax* (July 2017)

— INVESTMENT SYSTEMS TO USE —

— YOUR 401K THROUGH YOUR WORK —

What it is: Your workplace may – and likely does, if you're full time – offer a 401K for you to invest in: money is extracted from your paycheck and invested in your workplace's mutual fund where it is pooled in a family of stocks (instead of a single stock) which allow for growth but shelter from volatility[1].
Why you should use it: Secure, dependable, conservative-yet-fruitful, 401ks are not connected to the success of your business, and will not fail if your employer goes under, or if you're let go[2]. They provide a stable, dependable return that feeds off of the market's momentum – yielding sizable returns over time – but is less sensitive to the highs and lows than fickle single stocks and their ilk.
Why you should NOT depend on it alone, though: Simply put, by working with an investor who is searching for the best mutual funds out there, you can get a more aggressive return, but still enjoy the security and stability of a 401K[3]. Because of this, I recommend keeping and using your work's 401K, but only if you're also investing with a financial advisor who is seeking out returns over 10%, which are absolutely possible, but not heard of in workplace investments like Vanguard[4].

— WISELY MANAGED REAL ESTATE PROPERTIES —

What it is: Personal residences, rentals, or commercial properties – especially those with no mortgages attached.

---

[1] "401(k) Plan," *Investopedia* (February 2019)
[2] "401(k) Plan," *Investopedia* (February 2019)
[3] "401(k) Plan," *Investopedia* (February 2019)
[4] "How to Make 12% Returns… Forever," *Forbes* (January 2012)

Why you should use it: Whether it's your own home, a commercial property, or a rental, well-managed, well-kept, and well-positioned properties are almost always a sensible source of equity[1]. Unlike cars, houses go up in value with each passing year, can always be invested in to raise property value, and stand to provide additional income if rented.

Why you should NOT depend on it alone, though: Real estate is a game for people who work hard and love it; if you don't mind dealing with nagging tenants, leaking pipes, backed-up toilets, calls at midnight, renovation nightmares, and the hustle of the real estate racket, then you probably have the sturdy fiber necessary to be a landlord[2]. If not, then you'll probably only invest in your personal residence, and if that's the case, its equity – while nothing to sneeze at – will never be enough to fund your retirement[3]. Get and manage a house, but also invest in IRA's to really crank up your nest egg.

— MUTUAL FUNDS IN ROTH IRA'S —

What it is: A mutual fund is a professionally managed collection – or family – of diverse investments: stocks, bonds, securities, and more[4]. A mutual fund allows investors to enjoy the high returns of the market's general progress upward, while displacing the risk amongst dozens of investments. This way, while two stocks out of twenty might tank, four remain anemic, three skyrocket in value, and the rest steadily rise, investors will benefit from the gains of the three ascendant stocks and the eleven steadily rising stocks, while not being held back much by the anemic stocks, or jeopardized by the three tanking stocks. The managers of the mutual fund may choose to change the contents of the fund, keeping it competitive with others. This also leads to a great diversity

---

[1] "Key Reasons to Invest in Real Estate," *Investopedia* (February 2019)
[2] "Pros and Cons of Being a Landlord," *Small Business CEO* (October 2017)
[3] "Why Buying a Home is Not a Good Investment (It's a Service)," *Forbes* (July 2018)
[4] "Mutual Fund Definition," *Investopedia* (March 2019)

amongst mutual funds: while most either stay steady with the broader stock market or lag behind, many[1] (including the stalwart American Funds' Investment Company of America, which has averaged a high-octane 12.13% since 1934) have a history of beating the stock markets' interest rates (e.g., while the S&P might boast a 10% return, some mutual funds might render 12 or even 13% returns, or while the Dow Jones might be at 7%, another fund might return a 9%)[2]. A savvy investment consultant can help you select a mutual fund from the more lucrative options and ensure that your interest rate trends above at least 10%[3].

Another phrase you've probably heard tossed about is a Roth IRA, which is the type of account you want your mutual fund to be sheltered in. A Roth IRA is a specific type of retirement account that is tax sheltered – meaning you aren't taxed on your withdrawals[4]. This saves you from the often brutal tax penalties that many "not recommended" investment systems suffer.

The cons of mutual funds typically depend on the fund in question: some can be overly diversified, resulting in weak returns, and some can have higher fees than others[5]. You also have no control over the portfolio, meaning that if you dislike one of the stocks, you're stuck with in unless the managers choose to dump it. You're also taxed if you are invested in a traditional IRA instead of a Roth. So what is the solution? Make sure you have a great investment professional who has a teaching spirit and is eager to field questions, and tell them that you want your mutual funds to have diverse-but-high-earning investments, low fees, and Roth IRA protection[6].

Why you should use it: They're simple, elegant – conservative and stable yet hard-working and high-earning – and they are

---

[1] "Five Vanguard Funds to Beat the S&P 500," *InvestorPlace.com* (July 2018)
[2] "Dave Ramsey's 12% Return Strategy is Replicable," *Seeking Alpha* (April 2015)
[3] "Dave Ramsey's 12% Return Strategy is Replicable," *Seeking Alpha* (April 2015)
[4] "Roth IRA Definition," *Investopedia* (March 2019)
[5] "Roth IRA Definition," *Investopedia* (March 2019)
[6] "Dave Ramsey's 12% Return Strategy is Replicable," *Seeking Alpha* (April 2015)

exactly what they claim to be: no frills, no tricks, no plots. They can frequently earn over 10% when invested intentionally by a well-educated, high-octane investment guide[1]. Roths are protected from taxes if left alone to grow, are powerhouses of compound interest, and remain the backbone of any effective portfolio[2]. They aren't risky, they aren't flashy, and they aren't dynamic. As a result, they won't make you rich quick: they're boring, simple, and dull – but they will make you wealthy over the span of years. The downsides of IRA's are their lack of whizz, boom, and pop: lots of the systems described in the "to avoid" section are attractive because they promise fast, large gains if you're lucky (but they also pose to cost fast, large losses if you're unlucky...)[3]. Roth IRA's, meanwhile are steady growers, like planting a shade tree in the backyard and watching it gain a yard or two every year – before you know it, its big enough to swing from or fortify with a treehouse. IRA's are a steady-growing oaks of investment – the reliable tortoise who dominates the cocksure hare.

Why you should NOT depend on it, alone: Simply because it's wise to be diversified across stable, conservative, high-earning investments. So get and take care of a house in an ascending neighborhood, accept your work's 401K, and let these additional investments add to your portfolio's heft even while your Roth IRA's are the undisputed workhorses making most of your money

— THE 5 GOLDEN RULES FOR INVESTING —

So far we've talked a lot about the stock market without pausing to address what it is exactly. As you might know, the stock market is a financial system used by businesses to grow capital[4]. When a business becomes large enough, they sell

---

[1] "How Much Money Can I Make Using Mutual Funds?" *The Motley Fool* (January 2018); "Dave Ramsey's 12% Return Strategy is Replicable," *Seeking Alpha* (April 2015)
[2] "Why Mutual Funds are Still the Best Pick for Retirement Investing," *Dave Ramsey Blog*
[3] "Roth IRA Definition," *Investopedia* (March 2019)
[4] "What is the Stock Market and How Does It Work?" www.nasdaq.com (December 2017)

shares on the stock market in order to grow even larger, to collect new capital, and to use that to invest in their business dealings. When private citizens buy these stocks, which come with interest rates, they are helping the companies grow. In return for the capital leant to them, the companies provide interest returns which help grow their own capital, and serve as an investment for the investor which will ultimately be cashed for retirement or other uses.

If an investor feels uncomfortable with or unimpressed with a stock, they can sell it (ideally when the market is doing well – you would never sell low), or if they are attracted to the performance of a stock, they can choose to buy it (ideally when the market is bearish, or low: the best time to purchase[1]).

The stock market – which has existed in various countries and across the world in some form or other since the 14th century, and has been responsible for the spread of global wealth: the cultural boom of the Renaissance, the intellectual boom of the Enlightenment, the commercial boom of the Industrial Revolution, the technological boom of the Modern Age, and the information boom of the Digital Age[2].

When companies have the ability to raise capital by selling stocks, they can thrive and grow, and – in return – ordinary citizens can have their investments grow through compound interest. The stock market has gone up and down depending on the economic climate – sometimes dropping precipitously after a too-optimistic climb (called a "correction") but has steadily and universally gone up when looked at over ten year periods[3]. While some people think the stock market is dangerous or risky, history tells us otherwise: the people who are hurt by depressions and recessions are

---

[1] "Retire Rich: How to Buy Low and Sell High," *Seeking Alpha* (March 2018)
[2] "Don't Tell Bernie Sanders, But Capitalism Has Made Human Life Fantastically Better. Here's How," *AEIdeas* (February 2016); *The Relentless Revolution: A History of Capitalism*, Joyce Appleby (2011)
[3] "Recognize that Historically, Periods of Low Returns for Stocks Have Been Followed by Periods of Higher Returns," *Davis Advisors* (2011)

those who are either investing in single stocks or single bonds or other undiversified systems, or those who sell away their investments during a panic[1]. Hire an investment professional to manage your retirement, and although you should be involved in the process and ask as many questions as you would like, don't feel the need to micro-manage your stocks or obsessively check them every day or week or even every month (quarterly reports should suffice)[2]. As long as you are investing in good growth mutual funds with bullish returns and a diverse portfolio, you should never be afraid of the market.

Another way to curb fear with investing is to have a plan. Below here I've listed my 5 Golden Rules for investing in the stock market. Do these five things and you'll be investing fearlessly:

1. **Pause investing** if you're in debt and focus on paying off your loans; once you're out of debt, **focus on investing**.
2. **Invest 15%** of your income – EVEN if you have a 401K through your work. Let both accounts work hard for your future.
3. Work with a **SmartVestor Pro** – a proven investment advisor who focuses on educating you, not pontificating: if you don't feel like you learn from them, or if you feel like they talk down to you or brush off your worries, **dump them**.
4. Have your investment advisor find the following types of funds to invest in: **growth stocks, aggressive growth stocks, growth and income stocks, and international stocks.** Make sure you are **invested evenly** (25% each) in all four types of funds, and make sure you're getting a **10%+ return**.
5. **Don't fear** the market's highs and lows: no changes in the market matter if they haven't lasted for at least five years, so don't worry if the indices plunge in March; they'll probably be back and higher than before by June.

---

[1] "One Thing to Never Do When the Stock Market Goes Down," *Investopedia* (2018)
[2] "Don't Micromanage Your Investment Portfolio," *The Wall Street Physician* (September 2017)

— FINDING A SMARTVESTOR PRO —

You can find investment advisors who are expressly trained in how to guide you with the heart of a teacher, how to invest your nest egg evenly between the four growth stock funds, and how to find you an 11% return at www.daveramsey.com/smartvestor , where you can be connected to a successful SmartVestor Pro in your area.

CHAPTER 10.
— Understanding & Getting Insurance —

"[I] hate [policies like variable, universal, and whole life insurance] because they literally do absolutely nothing for you and they do everything ... for the financial salesperson... [Life] insurance was never meant to be a permanent need; it was meant to be there for you during your younger years in case something happened before your assets built up."
— SUZE ORMAN

"If anyone fails to provide for his own, and especially for those of his own family, he has denied the faith [by disregarding its precepts]." – 1 TIMOTHY 5:8

Maria was a stay-at-home mom with three kids and a good husband who worked in a Boston advertising agency. He was 27 and she was 26, and they were looking forward to planning a future once they got their financial sea-legs. In the meantime, however, they didn't feel confident enough to choose insurance plans, nor did they feel like they would be necessary until they and the kids were older. One November night her husband was with a group of colleagues flying in a small plane from a meeting in Montreal. The cloud cover was dense and the plane went down in the Catskill Mountains, killing all on board. Without her husband's life insurance, she was forced to juggle three kids, find a job working in a restaurant, and mourn her husband's death. A year later she was still waitressing, still trying to be a good mom, and still missing her husband, but their household income had dropped from $130,000 to $36,000 and it was all she could do to keep it together every morning...

Insurance is easy to gloss over, take for granted, or cut corners on; unlike utilities, rent, or mortgages, it doesn't obviously have an effect on your daily life until you need it, but it's critical that you take insurance seriously. Young folks, especially, might be tempted to avoid insurance because they trust their bodies, but it doesn't take a lot of logic to remind us that a slick sidewalk, careless driver, or unexpected diagnosis can devastate our lives and finances[1]. The purpose of insurance is to spread risk in such a way that we can be supported by the insurance network if we have an emergency, and the most important insurances to keep are health insurance, home owner or renter's insurance, life insurance, auto insurance, identity theft insurance, disability insurance, and eventually long term care insurance[2]. Not all insurance is necessary – some of it is silly, some of it is a scam – but I'll explain what you want and what you don't want.

— LIFE INSURANCE —

If you are single, have no children, or dependents, never, ever get life insurance until that status changes: it's just not necessary[3]. The purpose of life insurance is to replace your income for those who depend on it, but if you're a single, childless, 24 year old, having 7 grand in savings is enough for basic funeral expenses if you die[4]. If you're a father of three with a homemaker wife, then your death would be emotionally AND financially traumatic if you lack coverage. Don't count on your health or youth or luck: planes crash,

---

[1] "Why You Need Health Insurance, and How I Learned the Hard Way," www.moneycrashers.com
[2] "8 Types of Insurance You Can't Go Without," www.daveramsey.com
[3] "When Life Insurance isn't Worth It," *Investopedia* (December 2016)
[4] "How Much Does the Average Funeral Cost?" *Smart Asset* (May 2018)

cars skid off rows, and cancers metastasize on days when no one expects it. While the chance is that you'll live to a ripe old age, you don't want your spouse or children to suffer more than they already will if you die before your prime. You're the opposite of a single, childless person: you should absolutely, unquestionably have your life covered with a solid insurance policy.

There are basically two types of life insurance out there, one is wise and intentional, and one is deceptive and expensive. **Cash-Value life insurance** is something you want to avoid at all costs[1]. Sometimes called "**whole life**," it makes promises that it can't keep and hides a nasty secret about its stewardship of your money. Cash-Value policies attempt to juggle the roles of insurance, savings, and investment and results in an expensive, clunky product. The worst part of whole life policies is that they keep all of the savings it builds up after you die, leaving your family with the face-value of the policy only. So what was the point of all of those invested dollars? If you don't spend them when you're alive, the insurance company keeps them after you die. Bad deal. The alternative is **Term life insurance**. This is far cheaper because you're not pouring money into a hybrid insurance-savings-investment account, but it is only in place for the period you purchase it for[2]. While whole-life salesmen might consider this a weakness, it really isn't: whole-life policies are designed to be with you for your entire existence, but that's not what I want for you; I want you to eventually build up enough of a nest egg that you are self-insured. So what that means is that you should buy one or two Term policies in succession until – through investments, real estate, and savings – you've piled up enough money to fill your role if you should pass away.

If you do have whole life, be sure to get Term insurance BEFORE you cancel your whole-life policy, so you're no left

---

[1] "8 Reasons to Avoid Whole Life Insurance," *The White Coat Investor* (January 2012)
[2] "Why Term Life Insurance is Better Than Whole Life Insurance," *The College Investor* (March 2019)

uninsured[1]. Once the Term is in place, cancel the whole-life and you'll be set and won't be taken advantage of anymore. What kind of term insurance should you get? Approximately ten times your annual income ($500,000 for a $50,000 salary, $300,000 for $30,000, etc.)[2]. But keep in mind, this isn't permanent: your ultimate goal is to amass a nest egg for retirement that will ultimately make insurance redundant (which is why Cash-Value is a waste of money and time!)[3]. And don't forget that homemakers also bring genuine value to the family, so if you have a wife or husband who stays home with the kids, they should also be covered: if they were to pass away, you'll need to pay for services to replace them (a good rule of thumb for homemakers is $100,000 to $150,000 in insurance[4]).

— HEALTH INSURANCE —

For the time being health insurance – always a hot-button political topic – is a messy, complicated topic, so let's break down the basics and try to untangle the chaos that is health insurance. You'll usually have the option of either a **PPO** (a Preferred Provider Organization) or an **HMO** (Health Maintenance Organization)[5]. PPO's are designed so that subscribers are given discounted medical care. With these you have the ability to see the doctor of your choice without requiring your primary physician's authorization, you have access to a network of healthcare providers, you might not need a referral from your doctor to see a specialist, and you may be covered for medical costs that aren't under your plan. HMO's limit you to a network who provide discount care and require you to only use providers in that network.

---

[1] "How to Cancel Your Whole Life Insurance Policy," *Policy Genius*
[2] "How Big Should My Life Insurance Policy Be?" *CNN Money*
[3] How to Cut Insurance Costs by Self-Insuring," *The Balance* (July 2018)
[4] "Insuring Against the Loss of a Homemaker," *Investopedia* (January 2012)
[5] "HMO vs. PPO – The Difference Between HMO and PPO Plans," *Humana* (September 2017)

You need referrals from your primary doctor, aren't covered if you use a non-network doctor, but have lower premiums and usually no deductibles. So the short take is this: PPOs are more expensive but give you more options and HMOs are cheaper but restrict you to a network. Your medical history and needs might determine which is a better choice.

Another possibility is an **HSA** (Health Savings Account). This is a savings account that is tax-sheltered and used to pay for high deductible insurance[1]. **Deductibles** are the amounts that an insurance provider requires you to pay before they kick their share in, while **premiums** are the payments you regularly make towards that insurance. Healthy folks usually prefer low premiums and high deductibles because they aren't anticipating a lot of health needs, but still need to be insured in case they have a very expensive event[2]. Those with health problems prefer a higher premium (more out of pocket) and a lower deductible (the insurance pays for more care). So if you're in good health, an HSA might be a great idea, and you can either get one through your work or through an outside provider.

One of the first things I would recommend to you as you select insurance is that you consider increasing the **stop-loss** – or "excess" – insurance[3]. This is used to protect your from an unexpected or catastrophic event. So feel free to raise this, but if you do, be sure to never lower the **maximum out-of-pocket pay** (the company's out-of-pocket charge), which you want to stay high.

— HOMEOWNER'S OR RENTER'S INSURANCE —

If you live indoors you need insurance for your residence and/or belongings. Whether you own the home or are a renter, you need to have your property insured in case of an

---

[1] "Health Savings Account – HSA – Definition," *Investopedia* (March 2019)
[2] "Should I Choose a High or Low Deductible Health Insurance Plan?" *Forbes* (December 2014)
[3] "Stop Loss Insurance 101," *Business Benefits Group* (July 2018)

emergency. It's important that when you sign up for coverage, you have what's called "**replacement cost**," which allows you to – surprise, surprise – replace the lost property[1]. Make sure your insurance covers replacement and double check with your agent before you sign up. Something else I definitely recommend you have is an "**umbrella policy**," which adds additional security to your policy: this is intended to protect you from liabilities and is incredibly affordable[2]. If someone decides to sue you because they slipped on your sidewalk, the policy will absorb most of the cost and leave you financially secure.

— VEHICLE INSURANCE —

Obviously it is illegal to not have car insurance, but let's talk about having the right kind. If your car is paid for but old, cheap, or rarely used, don't waste money on collision insurance: the car will be easy to replace or repair, so save that money for something else[3]. If the car is newer or takes up a sizeable percentage of your annual salary, then collision insurance is certainly worthwhile. Just be sure that you have liability coverage in case of an accident[4]. As far as liability insurance is concerned, the common rule of thumb which I recommend is following the 100/300/100 rule: $100,000 for injuries per person, $300,000 for injuries per accident, and $100,000 for property insurance. If you have this in place you should never worry about being financially devastated by a car accident.

— IDENTITY THEFT PROTECTION —

---

[1] "The Simple Reason Homeowners' Customers Need Replacement Cost," *Insurance Journal* (April 2018)
[2] "Why You Need an Umbrella Policy," *Kiplinger* (July 2010)
[3] "When to Drop Collision Coverage: We Run the Numbers," www.compare.com
[4] "Insurance Mistakes to Avoid," www.consumerreports.org

Identity theft is a part of everyday life, and coverage for it is as wise and practical as having life insurance or home insurance[1]. If you find that your identity is stolen, contact the police as soon as possible and file a report, and execute a credit freeze (which requires writing letters to the major credit companies) until the issue is solved (after which you'll want to un-freeze your credit)[2]. The following process can take over 500 man hours of work and can be expensive, but if you have identity theft **restoration policy**, your insurance company will work those hours for you, and it is remarkably cheap[3]. Be sure that you have more than account monitoring: this just alerts you when things go south, but a restoration policy will do the hard work of fixing your violated finances and setting things right.

— LONG-TERM CARE INSURANCE —

If you're young, you shouldn't get this in place until you're 55 years old, but once you turn 56, this is a must-have[4]. Nursing homes are expensive, and long-term care will cover a lot of these costs. When most people worry about having enough for retirement, this is what concerns them, so let your nest egg go towards your dreams – travel, charity, family, lifestyle – and let long-term care insurance cover your expenses if you ever need to move into a nursing home[5]. This is also a delicate but very important thing to let your parents or grandparents know about: if they don't have long-term care insurance, they may be planning on living with you!

---

[1] "Should You Get Identity-Theft Insurance?" www.consumerreports.org (January 2017)
[2] "Identity Theft: A Recovery Plan," www.consumer.ftc.gov
[3] "Identity Restoration Versus Identity Resolution," *The Balance*
[4] "4 Secrets to Buy Long-Term-Care Insurance," *Kiplinger* (May 2015)
[5] "4 Secrets to Buy Long-Term-Care Insurance," *Kiplinger* (May 2015)

— DISABILITY INSURANCE —

Lastly, consider getting disability insurance if you have a very specific career (surgeon, singer, engineer, artist) that you have invested a lot into and would be financially devastated if something prevented you from doing that particular work[1]. If you decide to get this coverage, be sure that it is long-term disability insurance with **after-tax dollars** so that your disability checks won't be taxed – many plans don't specify this, and you could lose tens of thousands of dollars if you aren't attentive[2]. I recommend having 60-70% of your income covered, and be aware of the **elimination period** (the gap between the declared disability and the time when the insurance kicks in)[3]. A long elimination period means a long time without insurance, but it also means lower premiums, so keep this in mind when deciding[4]. Even if you aren't a specialist, talk to your family about the possibility of this coverage: if you get a diagnosis that keeps you homebound, you won't have to forgo an income with this protection.

— INSURANCE TO AVOID —

Don't bother with super specific types of insurance like cancer, accidental death, credit life, or mortgage policies[5]. These are redundant if you have good Term insurance[6]. It's not that these are nefarious or stupid or manipulative, it's just that Term will cover cancer, accidental death, and the rest. Save your money and take a deep, cool, sigh of relief: you're covered!

---

[1] "Do You Really Need Long-Term-Disability Insurance?" *NPR* (October 2017)
[2] "Is Disability Insurance Taxable?" *H&R Block*
[3] "What is Disability Insurance and Do You Need It?" *Dave Ramsey Blog*
[4] "How to Select a Disability Insurance Elimination Period," *LeverageRx* (January 2018)
[5] "15 Insurance Policies You Don't Need," *Investopedia* (February 2019)
[6] "Insurance Gimmicks You Can Do Without," *Dave Ramsey Blog*

CHAPTER 11.
— Understanding & Getting a Will —

"You need to have this stuff laid out in detail... tell everybody, don't leave the burden on your kids. Have a reading of the will while you're still alive..." "To be unclear is to be unkind."
— DAVE RAMSEY

"A good person leaves an inheritance for his children's children." — PROVERBS 13:22

When Lisa's grandpa passed away at the age of 83, it was deeply sad, but the family came together and supported one another throughout the week, culminating in a beautiful funeral service of sharing, remembering, and love. Her husband was shocked at how smoothly it all went: the trustee of her grandfather's estate distributed sentimental items as well as cash legacies to the family members along with a handwritten letter to each person. Her grandfather's life had yielded an undying legacy. When she asked her husband why he was so surprised, he told her about his grandfather's death – which occurred before they met at college – and how an argument over the sale of his house and the distribution of his assets tore his dad's family apart. Lisa suddenly realized that this is probably why she had never met any of his uncles and aunts on his dad's side, and was quietly and sadly grateful that her grandfather had been so thoughtful about his legacy...

ଚ୍ଚ

Wills can seem like a very middle-aged thing to need – kind of like life insurance – that you can do without until you're better off financially and in a stronger position to understand the scope of your life. Just like life insurance, however, this is a dangerous assumption to make. If you're over the age of eighteen – especially over the age of 25 – you need to look into getting a will[1]. If you're married this is even more important, and if you have kids it is absolutely essential! You need to have a plan for your loved ones in case you die unexpectedly. Remember: this isn't about you, it's about the people you care about. Please don't be selfish and force your family to have a financial trauma added to the emotional trauma of dealing with your loss – it'll be hard enough on them as it is without them having to make confusing financial and personal decisions without your guidance. But if you have a will in place (as you should!), you will be there to guide them even after you've passed. Also, keep in mind: you WILL pass – we all do. So this isn't really for "in case" – this is for "when." It WILL happen, and when it does, someone will have to figure out what to do with your assets, heirlooms, treasures, cars, house, children, and/or mementos. Don't let the state divvy these things out to bargain hunters: be intentional about who you think would treasure your possessions or steward your wealth (even if it's just $10,000, that money will be so much more of a blessing to a best friend, a struggling relative, or a conscientious charity than to the state).

    Wills and trusts are designed to help you steward your assets during your life, and deliver them to the right places after you pass away (which – again – WILL happen). Spending the hour or two needed to get a simple will is the only thing standing between you and becoming **intestate** (dying without a will and having your assets sold by the state). If you fail to make provisions before your death, the state will use the law to disperse your estate (laws differ from state to state), which usually means a spouse will receive 1/3 of the

---

[1] "Are you Ever too Young to Write a Will?" *FindLaw* (July 2013)

inheritance[1]. Things get way more complicated if you have children or aren't married.

Before you start a will make sure you have life insurance in place (see: chapter on insurance) – around 10 times your income in a Term policy – which is the first step in planning any estate[2]. After this, you can choose between three possibilities: 1. Owning joint assets, 2. Having a living trust, or 3. Getting a simple will.

— JOINT ASSETS —

Owning **joint assets** means that you have legally recognized a person or persons as your heir/heirs[3]. With this in place, your possessions (as specifically detailed) will automatically transfer to them at the moment of your passing. If the two parties are married, they often follow the **tenancy by entirety** option, which automatically passes forward the entirety of the estate to the surviving partner without dividing it to any other heirs. Joint assets, like living trusts, avoid going through probate court and are therefore cheaper than a simple will.

— A LIVING TRUST —

A **living trust** is a situation whereby you arrange for a person or set of people to manage your assets during your lifetime: you choose who is to be the trustee in charge of your wealth, which effectively corrals your assets under the trust, and tidily passes it on after your death[4]. Living trusts are desirable because they provide privacy (while a will is required to be read to your heirs, a trust quietly and discreetly manages the distribution of your legacy), it saves money (while it costs more to draft, it avoids going through a probate court (which wills do) and doesn't require those court fees), and it

---

[1] "How an Estate is Settled if There's No Will: Intestate Succession," www.nolo.com
[2] "Yes, You Probably Need Life Insurance, and Here's Why," *Forbes* (May 2017)
[3] "Joint Tenancy," *Investopedia* (May 2018)
[4] "Living Trust," *Investopedia* (January 2018)

distributes the assets much faster since it doesn't go through probate (it will take a matter of weeks to dole out your legacy, while a will could take months or even a year or more).

— A SIMPLE WILL —

A **simple will** isn't as "simple" as it sounds: to be legal, a notary must literally see it being signed and witnessed and must notarize it[1]. The will can be adjusted as often as you wish, but every time you alter it, it must be re-signed, re-witnessed, and re-notarized. As previously noted, the perks of a simple will are its cheapness and quickness, but it will bring with it a few downsides: it will distribute the assets slowly, require probate court costs, and be remove the privacy of a living trust.

— THINKING ABOUT YOUR FAMILY —

As you prepare to put a trust or will together, be sure to make a detailed list of all of your possessions and assets, explaining who is to inherit each item[2]. Think carefully about this: you might not care about something that could be a treasure to someone else (my maternal grandfather's Bible and my paternal grandfather's light-up swivel globe and his railroad oil can are precious possessions of mine that would probably been sold at a garage sale to a stranger if I hadn't spoken up). Have conversations about this with your loved ones: it will be awkward, but go ahead and acknowledge it ("hey, I know this is super awkward, but it's important to me that I have this stuff sorted out"). If a family is left to argue over your legacy, it can tear them apart; if you explain in legal writing who gets what, there's no confusion. And as you get older and – if you have kids – your children reach adulthood, you

---

[1] "Estate Planning: Living Trusts vs. Simple Wills," *Investopedia* (March 2018)
[2] "Making a Will: A Quick Checklist," www.legalzoom.com

should have a regular (yearly or every-other-yearly) family meeting where you discuss the will and make sure everyone understands what you are leaving to whom.

— PROTECTING YOUR DOCUMENTS —

Make sure that your legal documents are all clearly gathered in a safe deposit box at the bank and that your family and lawyers know the location (don't be sneaky and hide it at home)[1]. This will remove one extra layer of stress for your family when no one has to go on a depressing treasure hunt for your documents – let them focus on mourning you instead of stressing about your last wishes.

---

[1] "How to Keep Your Will Safe," www.nolo.com

PART FOUR
— Weathering the Fearful Storms —

Understanding and avoiding foreclosures,
bankruptcies, and collector abuse.

☙

CHAPTER 12.
— Understanding & Avoiding Foreclosure —

"People want what they want. And I guess that is a reason we have this big credit card problem and a lot of these foreclosures..." – CHRIS ROCK

"Do not be among those who give pledges, Among those who become guarantors for debts. If you have nothing with which to pay, Why should he take your bed from under you?" – PROVERBS 22:26-27

Kelli and Mark were in their late 20's when everything crumbled around them: Mark's business collapsed unexpectedly after he had taken out nearly $240,000 in debt, leaving them without his six-figure income and holding the bag for the business debt. Kelli had been working part time at a battered women's shelter, but had to leave this passion project to work as a teller in a bank while Mark – whose business had been selling high-end menswear to the social elite in London, Tokyo, and Johannesburg – found himself struggling to get up in the morning to work at a dark warehouse in a bad part of town. Their $300,000 income had faded to $80,000, and their $230,000 house – which they had planned on trading for a half-million-dollar mansion the year before – was now the only reminder of their past happiness. But within a year they were regularly missing payments, and after two months of missed mortgage dues, they were contacted by a lawyer: they were being foreclosed on...

ဆ

As I write this, foreclosures aren't as common as they were ten years ago, but they still happen, and many economists suspect that the United States is due for a correction in its housing market[1]. What's more likely is that a lot of folks are treading water – barely making their mortgage payments, or doing fine for a while, but praying that no unexpected costs come up next month – and that a sudden shift in the economy could send a tidal wave that would submerge tens of thousands of homeowners before they could recover. Dave Ramsey likes to quip that 100% of foreclosures had a mortgage on them and it's true: the only safe house is a paid-for house (see: chapter on mortgages). So while you may feel comfortable right now, it's important to understand what can happen if you get behind on payments, and how you can avoid have your house foreclosed on.

A foreclosure is a legal event whereby the noteholder of a property – usually a bank – can seize and sell the property if the "owners" fail to make payments on time[2]. Foreclosures don't just happen to people; they're gradual processes. Since it is a legal event, there is a very specific process that the noteholder must follow, which gives the owner a structure to navigate if they hope to avoid losing the house[3]. Firstly, they must give the owner notice, and if the foreclosure continues, the house will be advertised for sale for a period of time before being publically auctioned. That being said, there is no set period of delinquency before a bank can begin a foreclosure: while one owner might be foreclosed on after fourteen months, another might have it happen after only three.

— WHAT TO DO IF IT HAPPENS TO YOU —

If you are notified of a foreclosure proceeding, you must immediately begin working with your bank in an attempt to be granted a **forbearance**, which must be extended to homeowners who have the financial wherewithal to repay

---

[1] "Housing Market Crisis 2.0: The Jury is in for 2018 – 2019," *Seeking Alpha* (February 2019)
[2] "Foreclosure," *Investopedia* (February 2018)
[3] "United States Foreclosure Laws," www.foreclosurelaw.com

them. This will allow you to retain the house so long as you follow a strict repayment schedule, and is similar in some ways to a Chapter 13 bankruptcy. This is, of course, a frightening place to be in, and even with a forbearance you must tighten up your expenses, increase your income, and focus on getting caught up. If this is not possible for you, then you can reject the forbearance, allow the house to be foreclosed on, and make better decisions in the future.

      The most important way to avoid foreclosure, of course, is to buy wisely: find a reasonable house with a reasonable mortgage payment in a reasonable neighborhood. The 2008 crash was caused by creative mortgaging whereby people were allowed to buy houses that they probably couldn't afford[1]. If you can't afford a mortgage, don't let the bankers try to get "creative" with you: pass on it and find a house that you can reasonably pay off in fifteen years or less. Does that mean you might miss out on the biggest, prettiest, newest, swankiest house? Yes. But a staggering eight in ten Americans struggle paycheck to paycheck – including seven out of ten families living in that big, pretty, new, swanky neighborhood (in fact, 10% of six figure households complain about the same difficulties)[2]. Some of the happiest, most stable, most confident, most fearless people out there live in cute but modest houses in safe but humble neighborhoods, and some of the most stressed, most chaotic, most self-doubting, most fearful people live in those trendy McMansions in gated communities where they stare at their bedroom ceiling at 2:00AM, wondering how they'll make the mortgage payment now that their son broke his arm, the car got a flat tire, and their teenage daughter got a speeding ticket.

— SIX WAYS TO CURE A FORECLOSURE —

If you do find yourself in this position, there are several options available to you to avoid foreclosure. Foreclosures usually take place after a loan has been delinquent for 4-6 months, at which

---

[1] "2008 Financial Crisis: Causes, Costs, Could It Reoccur," *The Balance* (November 2018)
[2] "Most Americans Live Paycheck to Paycheck," *CNBC Personal Finance* (2017)

time you'll be contacted by an attorney via a letter, informing you that you have 30 days to become current[1]. The first thing you should do is contact the bank's Loss Mitigation Department, where they will help you develop a plan of attack. If you are able to get caught up within that time-frame, you will be given a letter of reinstatement, restoring your mortgage. If a foreclosure notice will be published in your local papers, announcing the time of the public auction. There are several strategies for preventing this from happening which may be applicable to your situation depending on the state of your finances:

1. You end the default by either paying off or selling the property
2. Some banks allow you to refinance the mortgage
3. You can arrange to willingly surrender the deed and be spared a foreclosure
4. Others allow you to modify the loan in such a way that you can make smaller payments for a certain period of time until you get caught up
5. You can arrange a short sale, whereby you and the lender agree to sell the property for less than its value
6. You can file for Chapter 13 Bankruptcy protection, which will allow you to keep the house given that you follow the repayment schedule

These options aren't always on the table, but if you talk with your bank's loss mitigation team, ask to see if any of these options might be applicable to your case.

In closing, please be conservative and wise in your house purchase: get what you can afford not what you think will be impressive. And if you do struggle with house payments, please consider getting caught up on your mortgage and selling while you still have equity: better to move down in house to something smaller and more affordable than to be forced to suffer a foreclosure.

---

[1] "United States Foreclosure Laws," www.foreclosurelaw.org

CHAPTER 13.
— Understanding & Avoiding Bankruptcy —

"'How did you go bankrupt?' ... 'Two ways... Gradually, then suddenly.'" – ERNEST HEMINGWAY

"Do not delay in paying [your debts]... Pay what you vow. It is better that you should not vow than that you should vow and not pay." – ECCLESIASTES 5:4-5

Although Mark and Kelli managed to alter their deed and avoid a foreclosure, they weren't out of danger yet. Their new, smaller house still required rent, their girls had medical bills, and Kelli's student loans – some $54,000 – were weighing down their fight against the business debt. By this time Mark had risen to manager at the warehouse, and had leveraged that promotion to a small role at its corporate headquarters. It was hardly selling high-end menswear (instead he was helping peddle above-ground pools), but the $90,000 salary, combined with Kelli's work at the bank, had given them a trickle of hope. One day Mark came home late: his car had failed to start and he had called an Uber from the parking lot. The next day he found that the car had been towed and that he now had to pay to recover a dead car. Hope and hoplessness crashed in his heart, and he began to wonder about declaring a Chapter 13 bankruptcy and whether or not it would wash all of this away...

ʚɞ

Bankruptcy is the last resort of a very frightened person, family, or company, and – like so many other financial choices – it's completely understandable why they run to it.

Our society has some flawed and inaccurate narratives floating around about what bankruptcy is and does. I don't think this has ever been better illustrated than in an episode of "The Office" where Michael Scott, the naïve but well intended boss, learns that his finances are a mess. Confronted with his middling income and his enormous Amazon addiction, he is told by Creed – a drug-addled, washed-up hippie with an ambiguous job, ludicrous work ethic, and hare-brained theories on life – that all he needs to do is declare bankruptcy and all of his troubles will be washed away: someone else will pay off his debt and it will be a clean slate. Empowered and newly energized, he strolls into the office with confidence blazing in his eyes and shouts "I… DECLARE… BANKRUPTCYYYY!!!!!!" Cut to commercial. Of course, not only is this not how you declare bankruptcy, but as Oscar, one of the company accountants, explains, this declaration will probably only make things worse and deepen the hole he finds himself in. Stripped of his hope, Michael runs off to hop a train and ride the rails but his girlfriend eventually talks him into facing reality (and presumably making some more rational financial decisions). Of course, 99% of people considering bankruptcy are far more informed, intelligent, and relatable than that, but they are still probably at least partially wrong about what bankruptcy is, does, and offers. Let's take a look.

— CHAPTER 7 VS. CHAPTER 13 —

Bankruptcy doesn't clean your slate, it isn't a fresh start, and it's not your only option if you're drowning in debt and desperation. Let's start with some definitions. A **Chapter 7 bankruptcy** is one which liquidates, or cancels, your debts. This is the resort for people with almost no assets to be taken, and costs in the neighborhood of $2,000[1]. **Chapter 13**

---

[1] "Understanding Bankruptcy: How to File & Qualifications,"
https://www.debt.org/bankruptcy/

bankruptcies are managed by a trustee who monitors your repayment schedule of 3-5 years: the debts aren't liquidated here[1]. Although 13's protect you from foreclosure and shelters any retirement accounts, they cost between $4,000 and $5,000. Many Chapter 13's will result in a payroll deduction which will be arranged between the trustee and the employer – you won't have a choice here. The bankruptcy court will decide what percentage of your debt you will need to repay – another area where you lose control – but if the schedule is less than three years, that percentage will usually be 100%, and even if the court previously agreed to, say, 80%, if your finances improve, income goes up, or payments are large enough, they can legally backtrack and raise the percentage. Declaring bankruptcy puts your assets in tremendous peril: although there are homestead exemptions which – determined state by state – protect a portion of your property, assets and income can be seized to pay off the debts.

      Bankruptcies don't apply to student loans, criminal restitution and fines, liabilities stemming from a DWI, or payments owed to the IRS[2]. Sadly, most people considering bankruptcy tend to have one of these costs in their life, and they turn to bankruptcy as a solution. If you have $170,000 in debt -- $90,000 in student loans, $15,000 in IRS payments, $15,000 in consumer debt, and two cars totaling $50,000 – a bankruptcy will still leave you with $105,000 that cannot be cleared away, leaving your credit destroyed, your finances out of your hands, and – worst of all – your ability to continue paying on the student loans and taxes restricted even worse than before. Bankruptcy isn't even possible for some – if not most – people[3]: you have to qualify for bankruptcy, and if the court determines that you can repay your debts due to your means, they'll send you packing.

---

[1] "Understanding Bankruptcy: How to File & Qualifications," https://www.debt.org/bankruptcy/
[2] "What Bankruptcies Can and Cannot Do," www.nolo.com
[3] "Who Can File for Bankruptcy?" www.legalzoom.com

So here's the long and short of it: bankruptcy is almost never what you expect it to be. It removes your freedom, devastates your confidence, cripples your credit score, costs money, makes no promises, and takes years if not decades to recover from. I never recommend bankruptcy because of its deceptiveness – it's a seemingly quick fix to a messy problem that leaves your life, finances, and future in shambles. If you have declared bankruptcy or are in the middle of one, you can survive it, you can recover from it, and you can start a new life with confidence and hope – even Dave Ramsey declared bankruptcy[1] – but it comes with a staggering cost and is not the tidy, get-out-of-jail-free-card that some people, lawyers, and late-night commercials make it sound like. So: can you rebound from a bankruptcy? Yes. Should you ever pursue it as an option? No. Find a financial coach like me who will walk you through the steps of organizing and mastering your finances so this never has to be a choice that you feel pressured into making.

---

[1] "Dave on His Bankruptcy," www.daveramsey.com

CHAPTER 14.
— Understanding & Engaging Collectors —

"The way someone deals with creditors says a lot about that person's character... The principle to remember is, to always run toward your creditors, not away from them."
– LARRY BURKETT

"Settle matters quickly with your adversary who is taking you to court. Do it while you are still with him on the way to court, or he may hand you over to the judge..." – MATTHEW 5:25

Using what she had learned from her job at the bank, Kelli dissuaded Mark from considering bankruptcy, and they plugged away at their debt. Eventually Kelli was promoted and Mark began to find contentment in his new job. Bringing in $130,000 now, they were able to pay off their smallest debts and feel the relief of margin as the monolithic debt began to break apart. But that didn't stop the calls... incessant, nightly calls... They should be used to them by now: it had been 28 months since Mark's business sank, and creditors had been hounding them for over a year. But nothing could restore their shattered self-esteem as they listened to the harsh, impatient voices on the other side accusing them of being irresponsible parents, failures at adulthood, and embarrassments to their family. Even though they could see daylight on the other side – they only had $180,000 between student loans and business debt, now – Mark quietly felt that each call deflated his resolve to keep working as hard as he was and Kelli kept crying herself to sleep when she though Mark wasn't listening. They needed a break, they needed confidence, they needed hope...

It's 7:30 at night, you're just sitting down to eat, it's been a long day, and the phone goes off. It's an unfamiliar number. What emotions do you immediately experience? Maybe it's confusion or annoyance, but for many people it's fear. You know who it is and what they want. You know that they're not calling to help you – they're calling to browbeat you. Maybe they've called you at work before. Maybe they've contacted your family members. That call means shame, anxiety, and abuse. But you're not as helpless as collectors want you to feel: you have rights and they are legally prevented from abusing those rights.

It's important to responsibly pay off debt with integrity and honesty: we're not about cheating our lenders or lying about hardships, but we still deserve to be treated with respect and to be permitted to pay back debt at a realistic rate depending on our means. It's also important to understand to whom you're talking: debt collectors are underpaid lemmings who tend to stay at their job for no more than an average of five months. They have no vested interest in collecting this debt; they're merely coached in how to intimidate you, browbeat you, and fill you with the fear they hope will motivate you to pay their agency[1]. Understand this too: these agencies buy debt for pennies on the dollar, meaning that they make a profit whether you pay the full amount or not. This isn't personal; it's a business transaction, and one which isn't very important to either the collector on the other end, or the agency they work for. You are one of tens of thousands of piddling accounts that they follow up with, and what feels like a terrifying freefall of emotion to you is just a light breeze to them. You're dealing with unmotivated, disinterested troglodytes who are reading from a script. Use this understanding to remove some of the pressure that they've been trained to applying to you.

---

[1] "Top Five Debt Collector Tactics," www.nolo.com

— PROTECTIONS OF THE F.D.C.P.A. —

It's also important to know that there are laws in place preventing them from doing some of the things that they do, and that you can report them if they violate these laws. The **Fair Debt Collection Practices Act** prevents them from doing some of the following things[1]:

- Calling outside of 8am – 9pm
- Calling without identifying themselves or explaining the purpose of their call
- Contacting you at work if your employer expressly disapproves of such contact
- Requesting a postdated check unless you have written notification
- Collecting an amount larger than the debt (what are sometimes deceptively called "fees")
- Contacting anyone whose name is not on the debt (either a debtor or a cosigner – NEVER COSIGN... EVER!)
- Harassing you, your friends or family (the word "harass" is a legal term which means different things from state to state)
- Using abusive or foul language
- If any of these are violated, you should demand to speak to a supervisor, and report the collection agency to the BBB and the Federal Trade Commission.

— NINE WAYS TO ENGAGE COLLECTORS —

When you're dealing with collectors, instead of avoiding them, there are proactive steps you should take to shift control of the situation back to you:

   1.   Don't avoid them; answer the phone with a cheerful, confident attitude (this is not in their battle plan, and it will throw them on their heels)

---

[1] "Fair Debt Collection Practices Act – FDCPA," *Investopedia* (March 2019)

2. Be polite to them even if they aren't polite to you
3. Carefully and cheerfully explain what you are able to pay; you're not asking if that's okay, or arguing what you do and don't have – you're TELLING them
4. Type out a script for yourself (and practice it so they can't tell that you're reading) and use that to boost your confidence. Keep returning to the script if they try to make you mad, defensive, or frightened. Stay cheerful, explain what you CAN and CANNOT pay, and then hang up on a pleasant note
5. Even if you can't afford a full payment, pay them something: $100 or $200 even. They'll always be nasty if you aren't making a full payment, but they're used to people either paying in full or not paying at all – this throws them off and cools them down
6. Start calling *them* regularly (once or twice a month) to let them know in advance what you are planning to pay that month (this gets them off your back and gives you confidence: you're not a criminal in hiding, you're a bold, confident debtor who is honorably getting out of debt)
7. Let them know that you're recording them, and proceed to record the call (many states allow this, as long as you tell them ahead of time)
8. Take advantage of **pro rata plans** to fairly divvy up your payments between creditors (but leave out **secured debts** – items with collateral like mortgages and vehicles)
9. Try to arrange a settlement; if you are successful, **get that agreement in writing**, otherwise it might as well never have occured

Finally, remember this: you are not a bad person. This is usually the thrust of a collector's call, to beat up your self-esteem, challenge your self-worth, and initiate your self-loathing. Reject this message. You are a valuable, lovable, complex, flawed human being, and you made a mistake in taking out debt, but that doesn't devalue your worth. You will pay off this debt and you will avoid it in the future, but we all mess up and it doesn't make you any less worthy.

PART FIVE
— Healthy Habits for a Fearless Future —

Having a positive, empowered mindset, an encouraging, edifying community, and a generous, charitable spirit.

☙

CHAPTER 15.
— Having a Positive, Empowered Mindset —

"Once you replace negative thoughts with positive ones, you'll start having positive results." — WILLIE NELSON

"I am leaving you with a gift—peace of mind and heart. And the peace I give is a gift the world cannot give. So don't be troubled or afraid." – JOHN 14:27

Maria, whose husband was killed in a plane crash which immediately transformed her from a well-funded homemaker to a single mom working low-paying jobs, was tempted to blame anyone for her suffering. It was her husband's fault for not flying in a safer plane or having life insurance; it was God's fault for letting him die. But this only lasted for seven months or so before she woke up one morning and felt the anger burning in her. In the silence, before her kids woke up, she screamed and raged and prayed and cursed, and when it was over, she felt that the rage had converted to a new kind of energy: she felt empowered by her expressiveness, and – in the cold light of dawn – sensed her husband in the room with her, almost as if he was laying a warm, protective hand on her shoulder. She knew that what had happened to her family was terrible and unjust, but she also knew that she was still alive and could still choose to get up and hustle. Throughout that week, the hot energy of rage still smoldered in her, but instead of escaping in self-pity and hopelessness, she harnessed it into hard work and creativity. She was inspired to help other single moms and widows, and before the month was done, she had started a business and paying off debt in shovelfuls...

Your mindset is the greatest asset you will have when beginning your path to a fearless future. In the 21st century we live like French kings: when was the last time that you considered a steak, chocolate bar, cappuccino, clean sheets, hot water, indoor plumbing, instant music, fresh vegetables, or electric light a LUXURY? In fact, if anyone felt like they couldn't immediately access one of these things, they would consider it an infringement of human rights and scream about oppression. "Chocolate is a human right!" If you're household makes over $34,000 annually, you are automatically among the top 1% most affluent people on earth[1]. That means two people working at Burger King – making 17K each – are tremendously blessed. Today more people globally are dying of overeating than starvation[2], and even while American protestors chant about inequality and oppression, almost every one of them has in their pocket a device that has MILLIONS of times more power in it than the computers that landed Neil Armstrong on the moon[3].

Indeed, they almost certainly have a better quality of life than any of their ancestors: they can have food delivered to their door without leaving the couch, can order books, clothes, and art online and have it arrive on their stoop in 24 hours, are able to learn the answer to almost any question just with a few flourishes of their thumbs, have access to thousands of hours of movies, shows, and documentaries for the price of one cheap lunch a month, and are able to terrorize and humiliate movie stars, celebrities, and politicians by using a few hashtags without leaving their basements, writing a letter, or calling a phone number. Life is luxurious and we often forget it.

---

[1] "America IS the 1%: You Need Just $34,000 to be in the Global Elite," *Daily Mail* (January 2012)
[2] "Obesity Killing Three Times as Many as Malnutrition," *Telegraph* (December 2012)
[3] "Smartphone is Millions of Times More Powerful than all of NASA's Combined Computing in 1969," *ZME Science* (February 2019)

So why are we so unhappy these days? Why are we so cynical and pessimistic? I know so many people who claim that the "game is rigged," that justice is an illusion, that oppression is rampant, and that the only hope we have is in electing a government which will legally re-rig the system so that the desired outcomes are predetermined: everyone will get a universal basic income, free health care, free housing, and free transportation, because what is the point of living if you have to work for these things? It's a human rights violation not to have $30,000 deposited in your bank account each year in exchange for having a pulse, and unless the government re-rigs the system in your favor, you might as well accept your fate. We are doomed – predestined – to suffer without relief, unless some political deity deigns to relieve our misery. As Buddhists await their personal enlightenment, Christians await the return of Christ, and Jews await the coming of the *Mashiach*, so many 21st century Americans await the long-desired deliverance of a messianic government to save them from their unhappiness.

What a waste of time and energy! Stop waiting for the same entity that can't fix a pothole (without six months of committees, evasions, and bureaucracy) to fix your life. You aren't in charge of what happens to you, but you ARE in charge of your own responses. Instead of bemoaning oppression, unfairness, and inequality, accept the fact that if you made some changes in your behaviors – at the very least – life could become more comfortable for you. By spending less, paying off debt, making extra income, and putting money aside, you might not be financially fearless in a month or two, but you'll certainly be making moves in the right direction, and three years from now you will CERTAINLY be better off (if not utterly transformed).

— MAN'S SEARCH FOR MEANING —

Victor Frankl, an Austrian psychiatrist who survived the Jewish Holocaust, was so impacted by his experiences and suffering in the concentration camps that he penned one of the most important books of the 20th century, "Man's Search for Meaning," which expanded on the lessons he learned about self-determination, free-will, and personal freedom. While some Brooklyn millennials and Portland hipsters might bewail their lack of free housing or free tuition, Frankl watched hundreds of friends and acquaintences wither and die under Nazi oppression. He was starved, tortured, humiliated, and broken down, and when he was liberated and restored to his freedom, it would have been utterly understandable if his response had been despair and depression[1]. The funny thing, though, was that he emerged from bondage with a positive, optimistic mindset and spent the rest of his life preaching the gospel of liberating the mind from negative thoughts. How could someone suffer in such a brutal and humiliating way and walk out of a death camp with a hopeful spirit? His response: choice.

The thesis of "Man's Search for Meaning" – grounded in a blend of Greco-Roman philosophy and Jewish theology – is that while we must accept that the world is unjust, unfair, and unkind, and while we may be forced to be physically, psychologically, or socially oppressed, it is up to us to make the choice of how we will respond: "Everything can be taken from a man but one thing: the last of the human freedoms—to choose one's attitude in any given set of circumstances, to choose one's own way[2]." Frankl noticed, while in the camps, that prisoners who allowed their spirits to be broken died faster, while those who acknowledged their physical bondage but rejected the option of spiritual submission had higher rates of survival.

You will probably never be imprisoned in a concentration camp, but you might face high interest rates, student or medical debt, foreclosure, repossession, bankruptcy, or collector abuse. Frankl's advice when faced

---

[1] "Man's Search for Meaning," Viktor Frankl (1946)
[2] Man's Search for Meaning," Viktor Frankl (1946)

with the hardships of life is not to choose despair or helplessness, but to recognize your freedom to respond. Almost all credible psychologists and therapists now employ some version of this philosophy in their therapy: people who have been traumatized, held back, or hurt should focus on their response to the past instead of wishfully imagining that things were different or resolutely blaming your enemies for your unhappiness[1]. It's terrible if you feel that someone has held you back, and I am truly sad that you were mistreated, but you are giving them control over your life if you blame them for your inability to craft an intentional life for yourself. Frankl wrote that "Each man is questioned by life; and he can only answer to life by answering for his own life; to life he can only respond by being responsible[2]." We are wrong if we hand the keys and destiny of our life to someone we consider more privileged or powerful; while life can happen to us, it is also true that we can happen to life.

— YOUR UNCONQUERABLE SOUL —

The British poet W. E. Henley famously said very much the same in his 1888 poem, "Invictus." If you would humor me, **I have a seemingly simple, but very important homework assignment** for you that will require only three things: your voice, some privacy, and two minutes. Find a quiet room and **read this poem to yourself in your mind**. Now, **read it to yourself out loud**, softly and slowly. Now – one more time – take a few deep breaths (fill your lungs with cool air, hold it, and now release it in a generous gush), and **read it out loud once more in a strong, resolved voice**:

---

[1] "How Cognitive Behavioral Therapy Can Prevent Poor Financial Choices," *Money Crashers*
[2] Man's Search for Meaning," Viktor Frankl (1946)

> Out of the night that covers me,
> Black as the pit from pole to pole,
> I thank whatever gods may be
> For my unconquerable soul.
>
> In the fell clutch of circumstance
> I have not winced nor cried aloud.
> Under the bludgeonings of chance
> My head is bloody, but unbowed.
>
> Beyond this place of wrath and tears
> Looms but the Horror of the shade,
> And yet the menace of the years
> Finds and shall find me unafraid.
>
> It matters not how strait the gate,
> How charged with punishments the scroll,
> I am the master of my fate,
> I am the captain of my soul.

Listen to those words: YOU are the master of your fate. Bad things will happen – they WILL – but that doesn't rob you of your ability to respond with optimism, positivity, and courage. Optimism doesn't mean being unrealistic; it means having a plan of attack and having faith that your plan has a proven chance of success. What do you need to do to start your plan today? What could next year look like if you take responsibility for your life and make informed, intentional decisions instead of blaming society, capitalism, the patriarchy, your parents, your race, your gender, your lack of education, your poor past decisions, your personal shortcomings, your anxiety, your hopelessness, or your fears?

And listen to me: these things can and DO affect people. Racism is real. Sexism is real. Mental illness, abusive parents, corruption, corporatism, intellectual disabilities, DUI's, criminal records, anxiety, depression, and fear are all real. But so are you, and as much as the past can influence the future, the present has just as much ability to craft a new road for your destiny. Choose to try. Choose to be disciplined. Choose to try something new instead of repeating failed behaviors and blaming the patriarchy, the government, Trump, Obama, racists, liberals, global conspiracies, or corporate greed.

It matters not how strait the gate,
How charged with punishments the scroll,
You are the master of your fate,
You are the captain of your soul...

CHAPTER 16.
— Having an Encouraging, Edifying Community —

"All the data tells us that your ability to be successful ... ends up being heavily influenced by who we hang around with... You *become* who you hang around with."
– DAVE RAMSEY

"He who walks with the wise grows wise, but a companion of fools suffers harms." – PROVERBS 13:20

Liam and Kaitlyn, our New Mexico newlyweds whose Valentine's Day dinner was ruined by worry, were starting to make headway with their debt. The only problem was that none of their friends seemed to appreciate their efforts. They acknowledge that they could fairly be called hipsters (she was an elopement photographer with intricate arm tattoos and he was a graphic designer with a man-bun and a well-groomed, Ulysses S. Grant beard) and the ethos of their millennial community was "eat, drink, and be merry, for tomorrow we die" – or, less eloquently, "YOLO." Their friends enjoyed spontaneous vacations, weekend trips to the desert, splurging on new shooting equipment, buying the latest technology, and not waiting to save before they tore off into the sunset... But it wasn't working out; three of their closest couple friends had gotten divorced, two had filed bankruptcy, and one friend had moved back in with his parents at the age of 31. Their friends seemed annoyed and angry when they talked about paying off debt. Some referred them to debt forgiveness programs (which have tens of thousands of applicants and less than 1,000 have benefited from it). Some hoped for a debt forgiveness jubilee alluded to (though without explaining how it would be possible) by socialist politicians. Others rejected the idea that it was either possible or even beneficial to pay off debt: "You'll always have it," they said, "besides; you need it for your credit score." Discouraged, Liam began talking about his worries to an older coworker at his firm who seemed kind, generous, and relaxed. The coworker invited the young couple for dinner with his wife where they talked about finances, worries, and dreams for the future. Kaitlyn felt encouraged by their conversation, and was excited when they were invited to a barbecue at the older couple's house. There they met new friends who were also kind, generous, and relaxed about the future – people with different backgrounds, ages, races, and jobs – who shared their values of positivity and responsibility. Kaitlyn and Liam started spending more time with these new friends – in groups and in couples – and less time with their more free-spirited-but-pessimistic friends. By the time they paid off their debt they threw a celebratory barbecue of their own with lawn games, fireworks, and cocktails. Everyone from the coworker's barbecue was there to celebrate, but only one of their old friends showed up – a recently divorced college friend who was trying to get his debt paid off. Liam was happy to introduce him to his coworker…

ಬ

I think most of you would agree that our society can often feel lonely. We are more connected than ever before, yet depression rates, suicides, drug addiction, family estrangement, hopelessness, divorce rates, and broken families continue to stay high or climb even higher[1]. Meanwhile, we use social media to excuse staying inside and avoiding people, binge watch Netflix series, rant on Twitter as if 140 characters make more difference than an earnest conversation, and stare at our phones more than our loved

---

[1] "Increase in Depression, Suicide Risks Linked to Simultaneous Use of Common Perscription Drugs," *Atlanta Journal-Chronicle* (June 2018)

ones' faces[1]. Several monumental publications – Robert D. Putnam's "Bowling Alone," Neil Postman's "Amusing Ourselves to Death," J. D. Vance's "Hillbilly Elegy," and Timothy Carney's "Alienated America" – should be required reading for anyone interested in breaking free of this counterintuitive cycle of lonely anxiety. They all speak to the decay of America's social fabric, our trade of community and existential meaning for individualism and egocentric "specialness," and the importance of diverse community institutions: fraternal orders, churches, charities, soup kitchens, bowling and softball leagues, synagogues, social clubs, hobby clubs, and philanthropic societies. Being around others feeds us (and I write those words as a consummate introvert), and restricting our interactions with neighbors and acquaintances to scrolling through Instagram is causing the cancer of loneliness to metastasize and grow[2]. No wonder we sense an increase in school shootings, domestic terrorism, hate crimes, political outrage, public humiliations, and "doxing[3]." Instead of rubbing shoulders, we depend on a dead, plastic screen to fulfill our deep, spiritual appetite for community and love. Ain't gonna work.

Beyond this, there is another problem that many people suffer with: they have terrible friends – or at least their friends are terrible influences. If you go to a friend with a fear, worry, or self-doubt, and their first instinct is to either validate that fear ("yup, you're right, it's just impossible for people like us to get a fair shake in life…") or to one up you ("that's nothing! Last week our pipes burst and we had to put it all on the card; nothing ever goes right for us…"), it's time to let them go and find better fellowship. You become whom you spend time with, and if your friends are negative, whiny, deceptive, entitled, fault-finding, grumbly, pessimistic, hopeless, or mean-spirited, your best efforts will often be

---

[1] "Heavy Social Media Use Linked to Isolation in Young Adults," *NPR* (March 2017)
[2] "Social Media Use Increases Depression and Loneliness, Study Finds," *Science Daily* (November 2018)
[3] "Why Has America Become so Divided?" *Psychology Today* (September 2018)

undermined: you can try to become better, but they won't surround you with the life-giving community needed to encourage you[1].

Instead, intentionally seek out friendships with the people you admire – not celebrities, but the people at your work, at your church, at your dog park, in your neighborhood. Ask them out to coffee or over for dinner, and **make an effort to see life-giving people once a week at least**. Open your house, your heart, and your mind to their influence. Ask them for guidance and advice and give your attention to their wisdom. Instead of griping on Facebook, mindlessly scrolling through peoples' fake Instagram pictures, or endlessly binging other peoples' fake adventures on Netflix series, walk outside of your house and rub shoulders with a community of your selection. Whether you are devoutly religious or not, try finding a church or synagogue or mosque and spend time with people worshipping there[2]. A good, healthy place of worship will often be socio-economically, racially, and culturally diverse[3]: you won't just be segregated into a group of friends who all look and think and act alike; you'll break bread with Hillary and Trump voters, blacks, Asians, Latinos, and whites, silver-haired retirees and mustachioed hipsters, bankers and bakers, waitresses and writers, struggling single moms and philanthropic millionaires. Get involved in a small group (worship services aren't where you meet people – find a weekly gathering of fellow worshipers) and start to meet the people in your community.

On his radio show, Dave Ramsey often notes that studies indicate that your income will generally trend within the average income of your five closest friends[4]. What this suggests is that if you spend time with people making more

---

[1] "Why Your Friends Can Make or Break Your Future," *Relevant Magazine* (May 2018)
[2] "Why You Should Go to Church (Even if You're Not Religious)," *The Art of Manliness* (April 2017)
[3] "America's Churches Are Becoming More Diverse," *Facts and Trends* (June 2018)
[4] "You're the Average of the Five People You Spend the Most Time With," *Business Insider* (July 2012)

than you, there is a likelihood that – through their influence – your income and prosperity will begin to rise towards the median of their incomes. Now hear me clearly, that DOES NOT mean that you shouldn't walk alongside impoverished folks, be friends with people with lower incomes, or spend time with the less fortunate, but it DOES mean that you should breathe wisdom into those folks but take your own wisdom from people ahead of you. If you want to be fit, don't spend time taking advice from out-of-shape people; if you want to be good in business, don't expect to learn from someone with a struggling, languishing enterprise. If you want to learn how to succeed in your personal finances, spend time with people who are thriving – who are saving, enjoying, and giving their money to others – instead of people who are complaining about the unfair hand life has dealt them. You become who you hang around with, so spend time in a supportive, encouraging community of positive, affirming people.

In his book "The Millionaire Next Door," Thomas J. Stanley breaks down the shocking statistics of what habits millionaires (people whose assets minus their liabilities equal over $1,000,000) cultivate, and who they generally are. Millionaires, it turns out, tend to:

- Watch very little television; they read 1-3 books a month instead
- Drive used cars, usually for several years at a time
- Live within their means – not taking out debt
- Value financial independence over making a public spectacle of status (e.g., big houses, new cars)

And so on. These statistic point to habits which are socially stable, personally self-assured, edifying, thrifty, responsible, and unapologetic. They aren't trying to impress people, use money to soothe low self-esteem, or build an empire. In fact, those that do tend to cycle through bankruptcies and teeter-totter between egoism and self-doubt. These are lessons you can learn from Stanley's book, but you can also learn them by spending time with responsible, generous, openhearted people who are living the life – and enjoying the fearlessness – that you want for yourself.

CHAPTER 17.
— Having a Generous, Charitable Spirit —

"To feel much for others and little for ourselves; to restrain our selfishness and exercise our benevolent affections, constitute the perfection of our human nature." – ADAM SMITH

"Good will come to those who are generous and lend freely, who conduct their affairs with justice." – PSALM 112:5

Lindsey, whose free spirit had been an inhibitor to getting out of debt, was finally on her feet, had an emergency fund, was investing 15% of her income into Roth IRA's yielding over 10% in returns, and was enjoying her money by travelling, seeing far-off friends, taking dance lessons, and learning how to cook genuine Thai food. But she was also sure to give: she tithed to her church, gave to charities with good reputations, and enjoyed spontaneously leaving large tips (every month she budgeted $200 for spontaneous giving). One day she was at the supermarket line and could overhear the harried single mother behind her trying to shush a baby, calm a screaming toddler, and wrangle a wandering six year old. Her cart was full of bargain and bulk food, her eyelids were dark and sagging, and although her face was beautiful, it was etched with sadness and worry. Without a thought, she told the clerk checking her out that she would cover this woman's expenses once they were wrung up. The woman immediately burst into tears and assured Lindsey that it wasn't necessary, but Lindsey smiled and said it was absolutely fine. While the clerk checked out the massive pile of groceries, Lindsey played with the toddler and talked to the six-year old, giving the mother a chance to soothe her baby...

Since you're reading this book, I'd say it's safe to assume that you are trying to get control over your finances – you want money to be a feature instead of a bug. What that roughly translates to is the fact that you want to have more money at hand for the problems life throws at you. Notice the phrasing "more money at hand." I say that specifically because to merely want "more money" is no solution to a financial problem. I have heard people – specifically one last night – who raked in $9,000 a month and swore they had no idea where their money was going. Or there was the woman married to a dentist with a $320,000 per annum practice who was itching to take out debt on a $1,000,000 facility, and was considering selling her quarter-million dollar home to help buy it. The Notorious B.I.G. quipped "mo' money, mo' problems," and while less money doesn't equate less problems, it is true that simply having MORE doesn't fix your troubles: you need to a have a new spirit – one of thrift and joy and generosity; one that saves and pleasures and gives.

— REJECT A SCARCITY MENTALITY —

So far we have discussed saving money and – to an extent – spending it (and hear me out: you MUST enjoy your money; to be merely thrifty without enjoying your wealth is to be a miser – a word too close to "miserable" to be taken lightly). But now I'd like to close the last chapter of this book with a very pertinent word: generosity. Financial stability is not about keeping money or lording it over others. It's not about fearing the outside world and clinging to your stash. Financial stability is a blessing – whether you're religious, spiritual, or a materialist, you must admit that this is the case – and it's not a random accident: it's an intentional gift to be stewarded wisely.

When thinking about friends who are bad influences, my mind quickly goes to an idea that some of my bad influences used to talk about – a scarcity mentality[1]. This is the idea that if a person has something that you have, you are being somehow cheated out of that experience. My former friends never used the phrase "scarcity mentality," but they lived it out by envying the wealthy and fearing the poor. Instead of viewing the economy as an expanding, accommodating landscape that can grow and offer vaster resources, they thought of it as a pie with a limited amount of slices. It is an attitude-disease that has infected all sorts of different communities, with splinter groups in almost every political camp.

On the right-wing it looks like people who wildly distrust any and all immigrants and fear prosperity in urban ghettos. In the ghettos it can either manifest as a distrust of the rich, or a disdain for (oftentimes Southeast Asian) newly arrived immigrants[2]. On the left-wing it can look like Occupy Wall Street – a nobly-intended protest that sought to tear down America's wealth and redistribute it without a thought for how NEW wealth would be generated (they were unwittingly planning on killing the proverbial goose that laid the golden eggs). Whether we're talking about nativists, populists, socialists, or communists, there are lots of people in America today who are afraid of being left behind, fear those who are arriving to participate in the American dream, and envy those who have prospered[3].

The cure to this disease is gratitude – recognizing that we DO live like French kings, that we HAVE been given a lush, decadent life to live, and that we ARE responsible for managing our lives and finances in such a way that we have done our best by what we have been given[4]. Gratitude breeds humility – the open-hearted recognition of our own

---

[1] "The Scarcity Mindset," *Psychology Today* (April 2015)
[2] "Populists on Both Left and Right Claim to be Fighting for 'the People' – but who Exactly are They?" *Independent* (August 2018)
[3] "Even in Better Times, Some Americans Seem Farther Behind. Here's Why," *The New York Times* (September 2018)
[4] "How Gratitude Combats Depression," *Psychology Today* (November 2012)

flaws and failures – and humility feeds back into gratitude (when we accept that we have been blessed in spite of our shortcomings). As the two feelings pour into one another, they will inevitably give birth to generosity, and while I advise you to cut back on saving and spending while you are getting out of debt, you must always be giving in order to nourish gratitude and humility[1]. These three emotions will help blaze a trail through your self-doubt and self-pity and light your way through the weeks or months or years it may take to pay off debt, establish an emergency fund, invest in retirement, and take your first steps of fearlessness.

    I recommend that, while you're paying off debt or stocking your emergency fund, you give away no more than 10% of your income, and while I don't insist that you give money away while you're getting your foundation set up, I highly, highly recommend that you do. This could be giving to a charity, to a church, to a humanitarian group, or – my favorite kind – to someone in need. But however you give and whomever you give to, make sure that you realize that whatever financial troubles you may be suffering, there are always others in greater need, and to them you are rich. Pampered, entitled hipsters drinking $8.00 coffees, using $2,000 iPhones, and riding $4,000 custom bikes might complain about being mistreated and neglected by the system, but that is probably because they rarely pause to consider how fortunate they have been: you could always have MORE money, but you could also always have LESS.

— GIVING WITH DELIGHT AND EXUBERANCE —

Once you're out of debt, funded, and putting away savings in Roth IRA's, I do actually insist that you give. It opens your heart up and fills you with a sense of charity and love that you aren't able to experience if you're clinging to you money like the pre-reform Scrooge. Larry Burkett famously said that his

---

[1] How Gratitude Combats Depression," *Psychology Today* (November 2012)

greatest fear in life was "standing before the Lord and hearing Him say 'I had so much more for you, but you held on too tightly[1].'" When we squeeze our money to our chests, our hands aren't open to receive what might be waiting for us, and when our hearts are closed to the people around us, they won't be able to receive the love that we might reciprocate through charity.

    Just think of what you might be able to do if you said "yes" to generosity: leave a $300 tip for the struggling waitress who delivered your burger and shake; anonymously give money for Christmas presents to a recently widowed mother; buy and give a used car to a cash-strapped college student; donate a new major appliance to a young family who can't afford to buy a new washer or freezer; gift a month's supply of frozen meals to a recently unemployed father; send your pastor to the house of a hurting family with $2,000 in an envelope from "an anonymous angel"; enable your neighbor boy to go to a summer camp when his parents couldn't raise the funds; buy an immigrant family new clothes, new linens, and new shoes; pay for one semester's tuition for a student at your church; donate $5,000 to a local fundraiser without blinking an eye...

    And none of these things are intended to be paid back: wealth is not an accident, it's a responsibility, and if you become wealthy, your responsibility is to pass your blessings along, and to coach, support, and encourage your neighbors to find wealth, too. While we have to remember the maxim, "give a man a fish and he eats for a day; teach a man to fish, and he eats for life," don't pass up this middle way: "give a man a fish to feed him, energize his body, and give hope to his mind, THEN teach him to fish, and to give fish to others." We shouldn't just make it rain money without investing in edifying, supportive, encouraging relationships that train others how to be responsible, but we should also be generous in our spirits and openhearted to people who are

---

[1] "Seven Practices of Effective Ministry," Andy Stanley, et al. (2004)

suffering: give them a break, and then – once they've caught their breath – stand beside them and show them how you yourself found a fearless future.

Now of course, all giving should be budgeted and accommodated in your plan (we don't just "let the spirit move us" outside of what we are able to offer). You can always shuffle things around (i.e., cancel that month's massage or fancy reservation at a high end restaurant so you can use that money to bless someone else), but we aren't wise if we just drop cash without knowing where it's coming from (nor do we ever use the emergency fund for giving). Remember that a person who saves but doesn't enjoy wealth or share it is a miser; one who enjoys but doesn't save or give is a hedonistic; but one who gives but doesn't enjoy or save is a nearsighted door-mat at the best self-aggrandizing martyr at the worst. So do the three things that wealth is for – spend it, save it, and give it – and when you give, give with delight and exuberance; spread your optimism and confidence, and live a life of fearlessness.

CONCLUSION

"Whether you think you can or think you can't, you're right."
— HENRY FORD

"For God has not given us a spirit of fear and timidity, but of power, love, and self-discipline." – 2 TIMOTHY 1:7

"Too many of us are not living our dreams because we are living our fears." — LES BROWN

"Be strong and courageous. Do not be afraid or terrified because of them, for the LORD your God goes with you; he will never leave you nor forsake you." – DEUTERONOMY 31:6

Lindsey – the free spirit with student loans – is debt free, loves the security of her emergency fund, and finds freedom in her budget (which gives her the ability to plan adventures without stress). She travels without debt, loves leaving surprisingly big tips at restaurants around the country, and spends her summers working with a girls' school in Africa...

Liam and Kaitlyn – the newlyweds struggling to pay off unexpected consumer debt in New Mexico – have new, better-paying jobs, already have a quarter million dollars in savings, spurn credit cards, and are grateful for their $18,000 rainy day fund, which recently paid for a surprise roof repair...

Carleigh – the waitress with an M.A. and $144,000 in student loans – started a side business, worked two part time jobs, and was debt free in three years. Her business is now a full time endeavor and she makes more than her gloomy, Marxist

professors who taught her that honest people can't get ahead and that student loan debt was a fact of life...

Jackson and Blakely – the young parents with a burdensome mortgage – went to marriage counselling and decided that their house was an attempt to meet an emotional need. They sold it, downsized, and are now very happy (and building wealth) in a cute, affordable, three-bedroom colonial...

Maria – the homemaker whose husband died without life insurance – managed to pay off her debts and start an online business (connecting widows and single moms to resources) that allowed her to work from home and make over $70,000 annually. She moved to a more affordable city, remarried, and recently had another child...

Lisa – whose grandfather's legacy was such a blessing to her family – isn't planning on kicking the bucket for many decades, but she and her husband have an iron-clad trust in place to make sure they can be a blessing, too...

Mark and Kelli – whose financial woes tempted them to seek bankruptcy – paid off their debts in three years. Kelli is now working a part time job at a yoga studio (just for fun) and can stay home with the kids, while Mark is the proud owner of a new (debt free) business where he teaches clients how to avoid bankruptcy, foreclosure, and collector abuse...

We began this book with six rules for finding your fearless future – one defined by confidence and hope instead of self-doubt and pessimism. As we end our time together, I want to revisit those six steps and what each one means for you and your own first actions as you move toward your fearless future.

STEP ONE:

— PAY OFF AND AVOID DEBT AT ALL COSTS —

This first piece of advice is truly the most important: nothing else can begin to work the way it should in your financial future if you're robbing Peter to pay Paul – if your money is tied up in paying for past purchases, preventing you from developing savings and laying the foundation to confidence and aspiration[1]. If you can't buy it today, save up and buy it when you can. If you can't imagine being able to save that up in enough time, why would buying it on credit be a good decision?

      I know many of you will still keep a credit card at hand to build your credit score. But why do you need a good credit score? Why? To be able to borrow more money. Why? Because you didn't just save the money – and also because you wanted a better credit score. Why? To be able to borrow more money. Why? Because you didn't... (you get the drift). So even if you plan to continue to borrow money, please remember that if you buy something in cash, it's a done deal – in the past – but if you buy it on credit, someone with your name and DNA will eventually have to pay it in the future, and by that point they might have something better or nobler to spend money on[2]. So avoid debt like the plague, and pay it off aggressively (stop savings, stop vacations, stop eating out, stop travelling) until it's dead and gone. Take on extra work if you need to, trim your costs, and then celebrate with a well-deserved financial splurge (paid for in cash) when you're debt free!

STEP TWO:
— REGULARLY OPERATE A SPECIFIC MONTHLY BUDGET —

Never forget that you have more money than you realize. Seriously! When people start budgeting, they always – and I

---

[1] "Don't Let Your Student Loans Hold You Back," *Huffington Post* (January 2017)
[2] "Learn 9 Reasons Debt is Bad for You," *The Balance* (December 2018)

mean "always" – find extra money they didn't realize they had[1]. If you start ordering your money what to do instead of taking your orders from it, you'll sleep better, smile more, and have more confidence. You'll start every month with a budget meeting (potentially with the free EveryDollar app!) that determines where your money is going that month. If things change, you can change the budget, but what you DON'T do, is just spend money. If you need to take 10 bucks from the entertainment budget to buy an unexpected meal because you left your bagged lunch at home, do it! Just be sure to take the money from somewhere. Having a monthly plan will ensure that you know what you're spending money on and why; it will give you intentionality, and intentionality gives you purpose, and purpose gives you confidence.

STEP THREE:
— MAINTAIN A ROBUST EMERGENCY FUND FOR CRISES —

A popular complaint about programs of financial empowerment is that they're unrealistic: the little man (or woman, or millennial, or B.I.P.OC. (Black/Indigenous People of Color) can't get ahead, and when it rains, it pours...[2] Only half of this – the last half – is true: bad, disappointing, irritating, unexpected crises will happen to you[3]. They happen to us all. Appliances break, car parts go out, speeding tickets are doled, taxes are demanded, plane tickets are required, wedding presents are expected, medical bills are issued, and accidents happen. But if you aren't in debt and your money isn't earmarked for demanding lenders, you can start the process of building an emergency fund of about 3 to 6 months of regular expenses[4].

---

[1] "5 Ways you Can Increase Your Monthly Cash Flow," www.StudentLoanHero.com (May 2017); "Practical Ways to Give Yourself a Raise this Month," www.daveramsey.com
[2] "Why Millennials of Color Can't Get Ahead," *NPR* (November 2015)
[3] "Is There Any Scientific Basis for a Belief in Murphy's Law?" *The Guardian*
[4] "How to Start (and Build) an Emergency Fund," www.bankrate.com (July 2018)

Once this is in place, you have a safety net for any reasonable cost (almost anything more expensive than that is probably an insurance issue); just think how relaxed you would be if you woke up tomorrow and had $10,000 or $18,000 that just sat in the bank and was never – EVER – touched for anything except emergencies (not for that car you want, that plane ticket you need, or that dress you can't afford…). You would never worry about being knocked down by an unexpected expense – annoyed, yes; irritated, yes; inconvenienced, yes. But an emergency fund stocked with a third of a year's costs turns a crisis into an inconvenience.

STEP FOUR:
— INVEST WISELY IN IRA'S WITH A GUIDING INVESTOR —

We likely all agree that we need to be saving for retirement, but now you hopefully have a plan to make investments that are both stably conservative and energetically profitable. By investing 15% of your take-home pay into solid growth stock mutual funds (evenly spread out over growth, aggressive growth, growth and income, and international stocks), you can probably ensure that you'll be a millionaire by 60[1]. Remember, a couple making less than 70K and investing only about $324 a month over 38 years can expect a return somewhere between $2.8 and $3.2 million[2]. And that's not taking into consideration raises and promotions. The stock market is a secure investment if you invest wisely and avoid anemic options like bonds, volatile options like single stocks, and crazy options like precious metals[3]. Invest your money in Roth IRA's with a SmartVestor Pro who has the energetic and patient attitude of a teacher, and you can begin to breathe easily, knowing that your future needs are being taken care

---

[1] "Basic Math to Get Rich by Investing in Stocks," *The Balance* (January 2019)
[2] "Retire Inspired: Take Chris Hogan's R:IQ Retirement Assessment," www.chrishogan360.com/riq
[3] "The Five Mistakes Keeping You From Getting Rich in the Stock Market," *The Balance* (October 2018)

of by the eighth wonder of the modern world: the dynamic power of compound interest[1]!

STEP FIVE:
— HAVE THE APPROPRIATE INSURANCE IN PLACE —

Having a robust emergency fund and a high-octane nest egg means that eventually you will be self-insured, but in the meantime, be sure to have the crucial kinds of insurance in place: a Term policy worth ten times your income (or at least $250,000 for a homemaker); insurance for your cars, home (or renter's), long-term care (not before you're 59, but NO later than 60), and long-term disability (if relevant to your career)[2]. Anyone over 18 should also have either a legally secure simple will or trust in place to make sure your legacy is distributed according to your wishes[3]. Having these extremely affordable failsafes in place add the final layer of protection to your finances and provide a trustworthy foundation for your confidence about and hope in the future.

STEP SIX:
— CULTIVATE A SPIRIT OF GRATITUDE, GENEROSITY, AND HUMILITY —

Most important of all, you need to foster a fertile mindset that helps you keep life in perspective. Instead of being pessimistic, having a scarcity mentality, or falling back on whiny tropes (e.g., the little man can't get ahead; the system's rigged; that's just for rich people; people like me just can't get a fair shake...), open your spirit up to hope and self-determination. Remember that while the world is unjust, and while discrimination, sexism, classism, and corruption are all very real, you are still in control of your choices[4]. While other people might be crooks, that doesn't mean you have to be a crook to thrive, and while people like you – whatever your class, race, gender, or orientation may be – might historically

---

[1] "How Einstein Would Manage His Portfolio," *Forbes* (December 2017)
[2] "8 Types of Insurance You Can't Go Without," *Dave Ramsey Blog*
[3] "Do You Really Need a Will?" *Forbes* (August 2016)
[4] "Man's Search for Meaning," Viktor Frankl (1946)

struggle with wealth, confidence, or security, that doesn't have to be you. You might struggle harder than other people, but you can still succeed if you make the right decisions and fight the good fight[1]. Resist the temptation to give up. Resist the urge to excuse your fears by saying "people like me just don't succeed." Maybe some don't, but some definitely do, and you can be one of them.

Also be sure to surround yourself with an engaging community of diverse, but likeminded people – preferably people whom you would like to model your life after[2]. Don't spend time with Debbie Downers except in that you are trying to encourage and empower them. Don't keep friends who are always complaining, gloomy, or pessimistic. Don't waste your time with people who don't believe that they are capable of thriving, because that means they don't believe that you are capable of thriving. Instead, spend regular time with good friends who are ambitious, generous, and supportive, who believe in your dreams and who have dreams of their own. And while you're at it, watch less T.V., read more books, find a regular community to pour into (like a church, synagogue, charity, or fraternal organization), and live life in bold fellowship[3].

Lastly, being wealthy and secure is not just a blessing, it's a responsibility. Be sure to do three things with your money: save some of it, enjoy some of it, and give some of it – and be generous with all three portions (don't just save – that's being a miser; don't just spend – that's being a hedonist; and don't just give – that's being a martyr). But of these three, be sure to pay special attention to giving. Broke people don't give to charities, give $300 tips to a frightened waitress who brought

---

[1] "4 Steps to Overcome Adversity and Amplify your Success," *Forbes* (September 2015)
[2] "5 Surprising Ways your Friends Influence You – Backed by Science," *Huffington Post* (April 2015)
[3] "Alienated America," Timothy P. Carney (2019); "Bowling Alone," Robert D. Putnam; "Amusing Ourselves to Death," Neil Postman (1985); "Top Reasons to Watch Less TV," *Health Guidance* (March 2016); "Why You Should Go to Church (Even if You're Not Religious)," *Art of Manliness* (April 2017)

them a burger and shake, fund hospitals, support orphanages, or pay for girls in Africa to learn engineering. Broke people can't afford to be generous – but soon you will be able to, and when you are, be VERY generous. As I've said: give with delight and exuberance, spread your optimism and confidence, and live a life of fearlessness.

You can do it.
You can have hope.
You can have confidence.
You can have a fearless future…

You can take one bold step outside of your anxieties and find solid footing in a new tomorrow that you design for yourself. You can reach out beyond the limitations of your worries and find support from a new tradition of good decisions and wise counsel. You can see it begin to happen today, and continue tomorrow, and the next week, and the next year. But you have to choose.

Choose to do it.
Choose to have hope.
Choose to have confidence.
Choose to have a fearless future…

ONLINE RESOURCES

EveryDollar Budgeting App
www.everydollar.com

Mortgage Calculator
www.daveramsey.com/mortgage-calculator

R:IQ Retirement Calculator
www.chrishogan360.com/riq

Finding a SmartVestor Pro Investment Professional
www.daveramsey.com/smartvestor

Finding a Real Estate Agent
www.daveramsey.com/elp

Finding a CPA
www.daveramsey.com/elp

My Recommended Insurance Provider: Zander Insurance
(Health, Life, Auto, Disability, Long-term Care,
Umbrella, Identity Theft, and more…)
www.zanderins.com

My Recommended Mortgage Firm: Churchill Mortgage
www.churchillmortgage.com

MUST-READ BOOKS

The average millionaire reads 2-3 non-fiction books a month and watches less than 2 hours of television a day. Instead of following the latest reality show, memorizing the jingles of commercials, or investing your evenings in shows that you'll forget in the morning, try this new ritual: every week night, after supper, put some light, instrumental music on (jazz, classical, ambient...), make yourself a cup of tea or coffee, get in comfortable clothes, and spend one hour reading. If you go through the books on this list, you'll literally be among the best-read people in the entire country...

ೞ

GETTING OUT OF DEBT AND MANAGING FINANCES:

- *Debt Free Living* – Larry Burkett
- *Love Your Life Not Theirs* – Rachel Cruze
- *Rich Dad, Poor Dad* – Robert Kiyosaki
- *The Laws of Money* – Suze Orman
- *The Complete Guide to Money* – Dave Ramsey
- *The Total Money Makeover* – Dave Ramsey

STARTING A BUSINESS / SIDE HUSTLE / DREAM JOB:

- *Start* – Jon Acuff
- *Quitter* – Jon Acuff
- *The Proximity Principle* – Ken Coleman
- *The E-Myth* – Michael E. Gerber
- *48 Days to the Work You Love* – Dan Miller
- *Building a Story Brand* – Donald Miller
- *Entre Leadership* – Dave Ramsey
- *Business Boutique* – Christy Wright

UNDERSTANDING AMERICA'S SOCIAL FABRIC CRISIS:

- *Alienated America* – Timothy Carney
- *Amusing Ourselves to Death* – Neil Postman
- *Bowling Alone* – Robert D. Putnam
- *Democracy in America* – Alexis de Tocqueville
- *Hillbilly Elegy* – J. D. Vance

ECONOMIC, POLITICAL, AND BUSINESS PHILOSOPHY:

- *Why Nations Fail* – Daron Acemoglu & James A. Robinson
- *Thou Shalt Prosper* – Rabbi Daniel Lapin
- *Freakonomics* – Steven Levitt and Stephen J. Dubner
- *The Theory of Moral Sentiments* – Adam Smith
- *The Wealth of Nations* – Adam Smith

PERSONAL IMPROVEMENT AND LEADERSHIP:

- *Rhinoceros Success* – Scott Alexander
- *How to Win Friends and Influence People* – Dale Carnegie
- *The 7 Habits of Highly Effective People* – Stephen R. Covey
- *Think and Grow Rich* – Napoleon Hill
- *The 21 Irrefutable Laws of Leadership* – John C. Maxwell

PREPARING FOR RETIREMENT / KIDS' COLLEGE:

- *Retire Inspired* – Chris Hogan
- *Everyday Millionaires* – Chris Hogan
- *The Graduate Survival Guide* – Anthony O'Neal
- *The Legacy Journey* – Dave Ramsey
- *Smart Money, Smart Kids* – Dave Ramsey & Rachel Cruze
- *The Millionaire Next Door* – Thomas J. Stanley

ABOUT THE AUTHOR

Michael Kellermeyer is a financial coach, publisher, editor, small businessman, and college professor living and working in Fort Wayne, Indiana. He and his wife, Kierstin, paid off over $60,000 in student loans over 18 months making between $40,000 and $50,000 at the time.

Since then they have built up their emergency fund and are deliriously happy not worrying about keeping up with the Jonses, and are instead using their income to build savings, enjoy life, and give to causes and people who need it.

Michael holds a B.A. in English from Anderson University and an M.A. in English Literature from Ball State University. He has taught rhetoric, composition, literature, writing, and logic for over nine years, and considers teaching – whether fiction or finances – his true calling. Since becoming debt-free, Michael has gone through Dave Ramsey's Financial Coach Master Training, and teaches financial fearlessness in and around Fort Wayne.

www.ingramcontent.com/pod-product-compliance
Lightning Source LLC
Chambersburg PA
CBHW021829170526
45157CB00007B/2726